LAWNS
LAWN CARE

Jane Courtier

Consultant editor: Catriona Tudor Erler

TIME LIFE BOOKS

Alexandria, Virginia

TIME®
LIFE
BOOKS

Time-Life Books is a division of Time-Life Inc.
Time-Life is a trademark of Time-Warner Inc. and
affiliated companies.

Originated in Singapore by Master Image.
Printed and bound in China by Excel Printing
10 9 8 7 6 5 4 3 2 1

School and Library distribution by
Time-Life Education,
P.O. Box 85026, Richmond, Virginia 23285-5026.

Library of Congress Cataloging-in-Publication Data
Courtier, Jane.
    Lawns and lawn care / Jane Courtier.
      p. cm.-- (Time-Life garden factfile)
    ISBN 0-7370-0635-8 (spiral bound)
    1. Lawns. I. Title. II. Series.
SB433 .C67 2001
635.9'647--dc21   00-053254

For PAGEOne
Creative Director Bob Gordon
Editor Helen Partington
Art Editor Tim Stansfield
Picture Research Ilumi
Commissioned Photography Steve Gorton,
Steve Wooster
Illustrations Karen Gavin

For Marshall Editions
Managing Editor Anne Yelland
Managing Art Editor Helen Spencer
Editorial Director Ellen Dupont
Art Director Dave Goodman
Production Nikki Ingram, Anna Pauletti
Editorial Coordinator Ros Highstead, Gillian
Thompson

Note: Measurements are given in imperial and
in metric (in parentheses) and should not be
interchanged.

CONTENTS

INTRODUCTION

A beautiful, velvet-textured, emerald-green lawn is the most important part of a garden for many people. It not only sets off brightly colored flowers and other plants to perfection but it is also restful and pleasing to the eye in its own right. By the same token, a badly kept lawn can be disastrous. No matter how magnificent the neighboring flowerbeds or shrub borders may be, the overall effect will be spoiled if the lawn is not up to scratch.

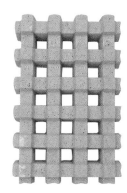

DIFFERENT TYPES OF LAWN

Grass lawns serve many different purposes. In formal gardens their strict geometric lines or ornamental curves set the template for the surrounding beds, borders, and hedging. Elsewhere their purpose is more functional: for example, to provide a leisure area for sitting or playing, or as footpaths leading visitors from one part of a garden to another.

For some people, the perfect lawn becomes an obsession. They may spend many hours and large sums of money tending the grass, nurturing it to a bowling-green finish, which is out of bounds to everyone but the gardener. At the other extreme, there is the garden owner whose lawn is simply a mess – bumpy and uneven, covered by as much moss and weeds as grass, yellow or brown in summer, and pock-marked with bald patches, which have been worn away by the passage of too many feet.

MAKING A NEW LAWN

Whether you have recently moved to a new property and are faced with an expanse of bare earth, or have admitted defeated with your existing lawn and need to start from scratch, making a new lawn need not be a daunting task. The most important thing is to spend time planning what you want, in terms of the purpose of your lawn, the types of grass that best suit your needs and climate, and whether to use grass seed or turf. With these decisions made, the preparation and planting of your new lawn becomes a straightforward operation.

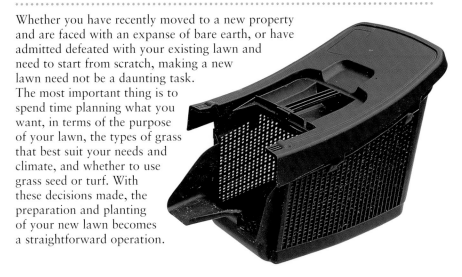

Restoring an existing lawn

Most lawns fall somewhere between the two extremes of a bowling-green finish and a weed-infested site. The grass is mown regularly, though perhaps not quite as often as it should be. It is fed sometimes in spring (though not every year), and weedkiller is applied now and then. It is a family lawn, and the children like to play on it – so there are some bare patches worn where their games take place. There are quite a lot of weeds, and moss is creeping in under the tree; in summer the grass turns brown but watering it is such a difficult job without a proper sprinkler – in short, the lawn is a constant disappointment, despite a lot of work, and quite a bit of money, being spent on it through the year.

Lawn maintenance

It is quite easy to change all that simply by having a better understanding of the needs of the grass. All aspects of lawn care are covered, from sowing or laying new lawns to the correct way to carry out routine maintenance, and restoring worn out and neglected lawns to health. If the normal grass lawn will not do, there are even some ideas on different "turf" plants, or creating a wildflower meadow.

Alternatives to a grass lawn

Lawns need not be grown from grass. There are many low-growing, ground-cover plants that can be grown to form a lawn. Those with aromatic foliage offer the additional benefit of a sweet smell in the air whenever they are crushed underfoot Equally, grass may simply not be suitable in your garden, either because of excessive traffic such as in a children's play area or because of poor growing conditions. In these cases, there are several hardwearing alternatives that you might like to consider. The thing that is most often forgotten about a lawn is that it is composed of living plants – remarkably resilient and long-suffering plants. Never let yourself forget that turf is a living thing, and give it the care and attention that it deserves. You will soon be rewarded with a lawn to be proud of.

Different types
of lawn

DIFFERENT TYPES OF LAWN

A grass lawn is a vital component of most gardens, but how often do you think of the many different functions that it performs? Before you start planning a new lawn, or renovating an existing one, you first need to decide on the type of lawn that you want, what you are going to use it for, and what best suits your site. You can choose between fine grade and utility lawns, and between relatively informal areas such as a grass meadow decorated with wild flowers, or more grandiose designs of geometric-shaped lawns enhanced by formal hedging.

A lawn is more than "just grass." The texture, color, appearance, and practical value of a lawn will vary according to the type of grass it contains – and there are literally hundreds of different species and varieties of grass to choose from. The mix of varieties that will be best for your situation depends on the climate in your garden, the requirements you have of the lawn, and the amount of work you are able to put in to looking after it.

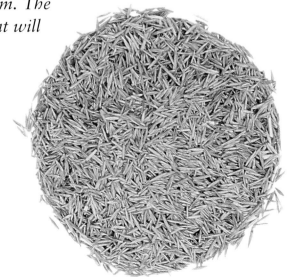

WHY HAVE A LAWN?

Probably the most popular home landscaping feature, a well-kept lawn offers a visual resting place from packed flowerbeds and eye-catching plantings, draws the eye to the sweeping expanse of a large property, or can serve as a garden path, a play field for children, or simply as a lush green backdrop to other garden features.

SERVING DIFFERENT USES

Once an important status symbol, lawns continue to be grown today but few people give any thought to the design function they want that swath of turf to play. Take some time to think about the role you want the lawn to play in your garden scheme, and then make it a part, rather than the whole, of the picture. A complete flat garden space devoted solely to grass is monotonous. Instead, reduce the amount of grass and use what you keep to set off other plants and flowers, providing a neutral background to highlight bright colors or bold shapes of other plantings. To be most effective, an area of green turf needs to be in contrast to other features. Many families want a grassy play area for the children, or even for adults who enjoy breaking out the croquet or

AN INTEGRATED LAWN
The gentle contours and even colour of a lawn are good foils for a soft planting.

badminton set for a friendly competition. Again, determine your needs and goals, and then design the lawn to meet them.

BUDGET CONSIDERATIONS

Planting grass seed or even laying sod is less expensive than putting in a paved surface or other hard landscaping. However, while the initial expenditure is relatively low, over the years the lawn will cost you far more to maintain than a paved surface, ground cover, or even a shrub border. This fact is all the more reason to carefully plan the space you devote to lawn, keeping in mind how much time and money you want to spend on it annually to ensure that the grass continues to look its best. Once you decide to plant a lawn, purchase the best quality grass seed you can find. Cheap grass seed is no bargain.

MAINTENANCE

Keeping a lawn looking green and lush requires a lot of work. The grass that forms your lawn is a living plant and, as such, has certain requirements if it is to remain in peak condition. Like all living plants, grass will only stand up to so much mistreatment before it begins to show signs of distress. Routine maintenance does not need to be onerous, however, as long as you plan ahead.

During the growing season most lawns must be mowed at least weekly. They also require fertilizing, edging, weeding, and often watering. Nevertheless, for most homeowners a beautiful lawn is worth the trouble, and there are cultivation and care methods that bring maximum results for less work. In this book you will find ways to grow the best quality lawn with the least amount of effort.

ENVIRONMENTAL BENEFITS

In addition to being an adaptable surface for a whole range of uses, expanses of turf grass provide many environmental benefits. For example, by absorbing pollutants such as carbon dioxide and sulfur dioxide, converting them to oxygen, just 625 sq. ft (60 sq. m) of lawn creates enough oxygen for one person for an entire day. Grass is a natural coolant. On a hot summer day, lawns will be as much as 30°F (-1°C) cooler than dark-colored paving and 14°F (-10°C) cooler than bare soil. Grass acts as a water purifier, filtering contaminants from rainwater and reducing runoff. To maximize this beneficial feature of your lawn, avoid fertilizing the grass with chemical fertilizers that can leach into the public waterways and pollute them.

COOL RETREAT IN SUMMER

FUNCTIONALITY

As well as being an important feature in a landscape design, a lawn can be a fun play area for both children and adults. It is a soft, impact-absorbing surface, making it a safe place for children to run around on. The springy surface is great for playing ball games, running about on, and provides a soft landing beneath swings, slides, and climbing frames. You can even outline a tennis or volleyball court directly on the grass with lime, sand, or kitchen flour. It will wash into the soil with the next rain.

Strips of grass can be used as footpaths, especially on slopes and awkward-shaped plots where it can be difficult to achieve an even foundation for hard landscaping. There are tough grass species available that can withstand being walked on frequently and tolerate heavy traffic such as bicycles or tricycles. On a hot day, you will find that sitting on a lawn is much cooler than resting on a paved surface, and in practical terms, garden seating is more stable on lawns than on gravel or cobbled areas.

POINTS TO CONSIDER

Mowing You will need to mow your lawn frequently in spring and summer, and as often as twice or three times a week for really high-quality grass (see pp. 60–61).

Excessive wear In areas of heavy wear, such as along a narrow grass path or in a children's play area, watch out for unsightly bald or brown patches and be prepared to repair them promptly (pp. 48–52).

Watering During prolonged periods of hot, dry weather you will need to water the lawn if you want to keep its rich green color throughout the season (pp. 66–69).

Feeding You will need to feed the lawn with a balanced fertilizer at regular intervals, otherwise it will deteriorate in quality (pp. 70–73).

Aerating and scarifying Compacted ground will need spiking periodically to ensure the turf is not starved of oxygen (pp. 74–75). You should also scarify annually to remove thatch from the lawn (pp. 76–77).

Weed control Weeds can disfigure the turf if you do not keep them in check (pp. 86–89).

Diseases Turf grass can sometimes (although not often) be attacked by a variety of troublesome pests and diseases (pp. 90–96).

Shade You may have difficulty establishing and maintaining a lawn in heavily shaded areas. Take steps to reduce the level of shade (p. 102) or consider a different type of ground cover (pp. 104–107). While grass is not a shade-loving plant by nature, some varieties are more tolerant of shade than others. If you have light or filtered shade, such as under a high canopy of trees, opt for a grass type that suits those conditions. Among the warm-season grasses, St. Augustine grass is the most shade tolerant. Other warm-season choices include bahia grass, centipede grass, tall fescue, and zoysia. Fine fescue is the most shade-tolerant of the cool-season grasses. Kentucky bluegrass and perennial ryegrass will grow in partial shade.

VERSATILITY

Lawns can be made to virtually any shape you require, and flowing, curved lines are much easier to achieve with grass than with hard landscaping materials such as paving slabs. If you want to change the shape of the lawn, it is simple to cut a new outline with a sharp spade or a turfing iron, and beds, borders, and other garden features are easy to add to the lawn, as required. You can also enlarge or extend a lawn, although this may be harder to achieve successfully, as new areas of grass may vary in shade and texture from the existing ones.

1 To make a curved edge on a lawn, lay a rope or hose on the ground in the desired shape, then cut through the grass with a turfing iron and lift the unwanted sod.

2 Use a series of wooden planks as a guide when cutting straight edges, standing on the planks as you cut to hold them steady.

CHOOSING A LAWN

Most of us do not need a lawn suitable for championship tennis matches, a putting green, or serious croquet. What we want is a turf that will grow happily in the soil and light conditions we can provide and that can hold up under the wear and tear that it is likely to get. Choose a grass type that is best adapted to your situation.

A GRASS FOR EVERY NEED

Among the tens of thousands of plants in the grass family, there are about 12 or 13 species that are suited to create home lawns. Within those species are named varieties developed by hybridists and researchers to improve disease- and pest-resistance, drought-tolerance, and to create other desirable characteristics. Qualities you may want to look for when choosing a grass type include shade tolerance; low-

maintenance; adaption to sandy or other difficult soil conditions; salt-tolerance; ability to withstand heavy use, particularly foot traffic; drought-tolerance; and pest- and disease-resistance. If you have flowerbeds or a shrub border next to the lawn, you will probably want to avoid invasive spreading varieties such as Bermuda grass.

The ultimate goal for any homeowner is to have a lawn that grows densely to block out weeds with roots that penetrate deep into the soil, making it more drought-tolerant. However, there is no one all-purpose grass that does well in

TRANQUIL FORMALITY
The trees and shrubs provide different shades of green, interrupted only by the earth tones of the house and urns mounted on plinths.

all gardens and meets all the different possible requirements. A grass that is ideal for a southern region may languish or even die in a northern part of the country. Research the best lawn grasses for your area just as you would study which trees, shrubs, and perennials are the best to plant. Check with your local Cooperative Extension Service and ask to speak to a turf grass specialist. This person should be able to advise about which grass varieties are best suited to your region, and even help you to narrow down your choice further by discussing the growing conditions you will be providing.

SEASONAL GRASSES

In addition to whether they are fine, medium, or coarse textured (see p. 15), grasses are divided into two main categories: warm season and cool season.

Generally cool-season grasses suit climates where temperatures fall below freezing. These grasses grow best in spring and fall, entering a dormancy period during winter and through hot, dry spells in summer. When dormant, the grasses turn brown and look dead, but once the weather cools down in the fall (or warms up in spring) and the rains return, they will spring back to life and turn vibrant green once more. Regular irrigation will deter these lawns from entering dormancy during summer.

Warm-season grasses are suited to growing in warm climates where the temperatures generally stay above freezing. These grasses fall dormant during winter. To keep a green lawn throughout the year, homeowners overseed their warm-season lawns with annual or perennial ryegrass or fescue in the fall.

CREATING CONTRASTS

As long as the site is not too small, there is no reason why you shouldn't combine different types of grass in the same garden. Different effects can also be achieved by combining grass with hard surfacing materials.

• A wide, mowed grass path through an area of rough grass and wild flowers can be extremely effective.

• The velvet texture of a pristine lawn will produce a pleasing contrast within a larger area of slightly longer, rougher-textured grass.

• Combining grass with small, evenly shaped pavers, perhaps across a lawn or between flowerbeds, will provide a practical and attractive pathway.

FUN WITH GRASS
There is no need to confine yourself to a flat lawn in a regular shape when using turf. Grass can be molded to a variety of shapes, as demonstrated by this quirky garden table and mushroom-shaped stools upholstered in grass.

ROUGH GRASS

In certain areas of the garden –
such as on steeply sloping banks –
a regularly mowed lawn may not be
practical, or you may prefer to leave
an informal area of rough grass to
form a wildflower meadow or wild
garden (see pp. 110–111). The grass
will still need cutting, although much
less regularly than a closely mowed
lawn. Normally two or three cuts a
year in summer are all that is
required. The appearance of the grass
after mowing is not so important, so
you may choose a lawnmower for
speed and ease of use rather than the
finish it gives. It is also unnecessary
to collect grass clippings.

Rough grass is particularly
appropriate beneath groups of trees,
and it looks very attractive when
planted with naturalized bulbs.

Spring bulbs such as daffodils are the
most commonly seen, although you
can also use bulbs that flower in
summer and fall to good effect. On a
small scale, dwarf species bulbs look
particularly charming, but it is better
to choose strong-growing, vigorous
varieties if you want them to
compete successfully with the grass.

The timing of mowing is critical,
according to the type of bulbs
planted. To ensure that spring bulbs
produce a good performance season
after season, you need to allow the
foliage to remain on the plants for
six weeks after flowering, which
means that you cannot mow the
grass during this time. For bulbs that
flower in the fall, do not mow once
the bulb's shoots have started to push
through the soil in late summer.

NATURALIZING BULBS

Plant bulbs suitable for naturalizing
in fall or spring, depending on
species, include *Allium, Anemone,*

*Crocus, Erythronium, Fritillaria,
Leucojum, Muscari, Narcissus,
Ornithogalum, Scilla,* and *Tulipa.*

1 For the most natural appearance
scatter a handful of bulbs (here,
Crocus) at random across an area of
grass, planting them where they fall.

2 Make a hole in the turf for each
bulb to the required depth. Add a
little bonemeal before planting, then
firm the soil and turf around the bulb.

FINE- OR COARSE-TEXTURED LAWN?

GRASS TYPE	TEXTURE	CHARACTERISTICS
Tall fescue Cool season Zones 5–7	Wide, coarse blades	Vigorous, tough, clump-forming grass; low-maintenance
Creeping red fescue Cool season Zones 2–8	Fine blades	Shade tolerant; drought resistant; dislikes heavy foot traffic
Perennial ryegrass Cool season Zones 3–7	Wide, coarse blades; newer cultivars have finer texture	Tolerates foot traffic; insect- and disease-resistant
Kentucky bluegrass Cool season Zones 1–6	Fine blades	Dislikes excessive foot traffic; needs full sun
Blue Grama grass Warm season Zones 3–10	Narrow blades, but not smooth texture	Tolerates foot traffic, light shade, and cold; drought-resistant
Buffalo grass Warm season Zones 3–9	Fine blades	Tough grass, drought-, pest-, and disease-resistant; tolerates cold
Bermuda grass Warm season Zones 7–10+	Medium to fine texture	Disease-resistant; tolerates drought, foot traffic, and salt
Centipede grass Warm season Zones 7–9	Coarse blades	Dense, vigorous; disease-resistant; tolerates light shade
Bahia grass Warm season Zones 9–11	Coarse, tough blades	Survives sandy and infertile soil; tolerates shade, foot traffic
St. Augustine grass Warm season Zones 9–11	Coarse, thick blades	Resists salt spray and wind; likes sandy, moist soil; disease-prone
Zoysia grass **'Emerald'** Warm season Zones 6–9	Fine blades	Slow-growing; drought-resistant; prone to thatch; not suited to overseeding in winter

LAWN GRASS VARIETIES

Opt for cool-season grass if you live where winter temperatures fall below freezing. While you can grow just one variety, most homeowners choose a mixture of cool-season grasses to combine the strengths of different species and minimize the weaknesses. Warm-season grasses are ideal for mild climates. Generally they are not mixed because they do not blend into each other and create a patched effect.

CHOOSING LAWN SEED

The two main considerations when choosing grasses are whether a fine or utility lawn is required, and what type of climate the grass is to grow in. Climate may be divided into cool, temperate zones and warm zones. Cool-season grasses grow best at 59–75°F (15–24°C); warm-season grasses have an optimum growing temperature of 80–90°F (27–32°C).

COOL-SEASON GRASSES

Fine fescue (*Festuca* species), zones 2–7 Includes chewings, creeping red, and hard fescue. All of these grasses mix well with perennial rye and bluegrass, adding drought and shade tolerance. They are prone to fungal diseases in hot humidity, and do not take heavy foot traffic.

Kentucky bluegrass (*Poa pratensis*), zones 3–7 A fine-textured grass that tolerates drought and temperature extremes, however, it cannot withstand heavy foot traffic. Blend at least three varieties to take advantage of differing disease and pest resistance. There are more than 100 cultivars

from which to choose. Your local nursery or Cooperative Extension Service should advise you on the best varieties for your region.

Perennial ryegrass (*Lolium perenne*), zones 3–7 Excellent for all-purpose lawns, the endophyte-enhanced cultivars have increased disease- and pest-resistance (see p. 18). This grass will grow in difficult, compacted soils, and requires only light feeding. It is best suited to areas where winters are mild and summers cool and moist. 'Derby' and 'Pennfine' tolerate heat and drought well; choose 'Regal' for cold tolerance.

Tall fescue (*Festuca arundinacea*), zones 2–7 Clump-forming, sturdy grass that is suitable for play and utility areas. Vigorous growth crowds out weeds as well as less aggressive fine-textured grasses. Requires little maintenance and is drought-tolerant. Pass over the old 'Kentucky 31' and 'Alta' hybrids in favor of improved varieties that are more disease- and insect-resistant.

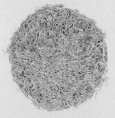

LUXURY GRADE SEED

WARM-SEASON GRASSES

Bahia grass *(Paspalum notatum)*, zones 7–10
A tough, coarse grass that needs sharp mowing blades, it is nevertheless a good utilitarian choice. Grows on infertile, sandy soil, withstands drought and neglect. Grows poorly where soil is alkaline or where salt spray is an issue. It tolerates both shade and foot traffic.

Bermuda grass *(Cynodon* species), zones 7–10
Vigorous, spreading grass that tolerates heat and drought as well as salty soils and foot traffic. Must be edged regularly to prevent invasive spreading. Also prone to thatch. Look for improved cultivars such as 'Guymon,' 'Cheyenne,' and 'Sundevil.' Overseed in winter when the grass turns brown.

Blue Grama grass *(Bouteloua gracilis)*, zones 3–10
This grass suits warm and cold climates. It takes foot traffic, drought (turns brown in dry weather), and alkaline conditions. Low maintenance and almost insect - and disease-free, mix it with buffalo grass for the best of both species.

Buffalo grass *(Buchloe dactyloides)*, zones 3–9
Native to the US Great Plains, this is a heat- and drought-tolerant grass that grows best in full sun in well-drained loam. It will languish in wet, poorly drained soil or sandy conditions. A very slow grower, it requires virtually no mowing since its ultimate height is only 4–6 in (10–15 cm). Select improved cultivars such as '609', 'Prairie', 'Plains', 'Cody', and 'Topgun.'

Carpet grass *(Axonopus affinis)*, zones 8–9
A utilitarian, cold-sensitive grass for the deep south where nothing else will grow. It is a coarse, spreading species that turns brown in winter. Disease- and pest-resistant, carpet grass requires lots of moisture and grows best in sandy, slightly acid soil in full sun. It requires only light feeding.

Centipede grass *(Eremochloa ophiuroides)*, zones 7–9
Prefers well-drained soil, although it is not finicky about type and tolerates acidic conditions. A slow grower and light feeder (although it can suffer from iron deficiency), it requires less mowing than some species and less maintenance. Its normal color is yellow-green; fertilizing to improve color encourages thatch. Can take only light traffic.

St. Augustine *(Stenotaphrum secundatum)*, zones 8–10
Quite hard wearing and shade-tolerant, it also accepts salt spray and wind. Unfortunately, it goes dormant when not watered, tends to develop thatch, and is prone to chinch bugs ('Floratam,' 'Floralawn,' and 'FX-10' are bred to resist chinch bugs) and to St. Augustine grass decline (SAD) virus.

Zoysia grass *(Zoysia* species), zones 6–9
Ideal for transitional areas between hot and cold climates. Slow growing, it is drought-resistant and produces a thick turf that competes well with weeds.

UTILITY GRADE SEED

WHAT TO LOOK FOR

E veryone loves a bargain; however opting for inexpensive turf or grass seed is not a good way to save money. The seed may cost less but the seeds have a low germination rate as well as a high proportion of weed seeds and inert matter. Pound for pound, you may actually pay more for the "cheaper" package than a more expensive counterpart. You get what you pay for.

UNDERSTANDING THE LABEL

Check for the following information:

■ **Percent of pure seed** The label should list each type of grass in the package and percentage of each, based on weight, not quantity. For example, a 50% blend of bluegrass and fine fescue is made up of two-thirds bluegrass seed and one-third fescue, since bluegrass seed is much lighter than fescue. Avoid mixes with a total of less than 80% desirable permanent lawn species. Unless overseeding a warm-season lawn for winter, look for a content of less than 3–5% of annual grasses. Avoid seed mixes carrying the initials "VNS" (this means "variety not stated").

■ **Cultivar names** Many of the new cultivars or trade-named grasses are better than the plain species, and are worth paying more for. If cultivars are not listed, the seed is probably just the species or an older variety that is not worth mentioning.

■ **Germination** The percentage of live or viable seed. Expect a germination rate of at least 85%.

■ **Weed seeds** Accept no more than 0.5% weed seed by weight. Look for the guarantee of "No noxious weeds."

■ **Test date** The date the seeds were tested for viability. Avoid seed that was tested more than 9–12 months before the purchase date.

■ **Endophyte enhanced** Endophytes are small fungi that are deadly to many grass insects. Make sure there is a minimum of 50% endophyte-enhanced seed.

BUYING SOD
Look for a tightly knit "backcloth" of moist soil and an even distribution of grass tufts. Stack the sod in a pyramid in a shaded area, and cover with a blanket to conserve moisture.

Making a new lawn

2

Making a New Lawn

Whether you are starting with a new plot or replacing an existing lawn, making a new lawn is an opportunity to choose a variety that best suits your climate and needs.

Before planting, take the time to collect soil samples and have them evaluated by a professional laboratory, whose report will give a comprehensive breakdown of the pH and nutrients in the soil as well as recommendations for soil improvers.

Look for grass varieties that suit your region and climate as well as any new cultivar introductions that feature superior growth habit, texture, drought-tolerance, cold- or heat-hardiness, or pest- and disease-resistance. Planting a new lawn is a long-term investment in the health of your garden. It is well worth taking the time and effort up front to make sure that your investment pays you good dividends.

SEED OR SOD?

There are two primary ways of establishing a lawn: one is to plant seeds, the other is to lay sod. Each method has its benefits and disadvantages. Which approach you choose will depend on factors such as your budget, how quickly you need an established lawn, and the selection of grass you want. In southern regions, you can also plant a lawn using plugs or sprigs (see p. 21).

2

LAWNS FROM SEED

ADVANTAGES

Economy Seed is less expensive than sod, but invest in the best-quality seed you can find. Cheap seed has a low germination rate, more inert matter or filler, and a high percentage of weed seeds. Always buy fresh seed.

For beginners Seeding is quite an easy job, and involves less work than laying sod or planting sprigs or plugs.

More selection You will find a far wider choice of improved named varieties in grass seeds than in turf grass sod.

DISADVANTAGES

Slow to establish It takes up to several weeks for seeds to germinate, and many months before the lawn can stand up to normal use.

Long-term care required Once sown, the seeds must be kept moist until they germinate, but hard rain can wash them away. Seeds need to be protected from birds and pedestrians.

Weeds Invariably, weeds can sprout and take hold before the grass fills in.

PROTECTIVE NETTING

Other planting methods

As an alternative to seed and sod, warm-season grasses are available as sprigs or plugs.

■ **Plugs** These are small strips or cubes of sod 2–3 in (5–8 cm) in diameter. Generally they are sold in flats or trays of 12 or 24 plugs. Plant plugs as you would any small plant, spacing them at recommended intervals. Bermuda grass plugs generally are planted 4–12 in (10–30 cm) apart; centipede, St. Augustine, and Zoysia grass all can be spaced 6–12 in (15–30 cm) apart.

■ **Sprigs** Consisting of cut-up lengths of rhizomes or stolens (the aboveground and underground runners characteristic of many warm-season grasses), each sprig bears two or four growing nodes from which the new grass sprouts. They are most often sold by the bushel. About four or five bushels of sprigs are needed to plant an area of 1,000 sq. ft (90 sq. m) of lawn. Plant the sprigs by broadcasting them evenly across the space and then press them firmly into the soil or bury them in shallow furrows.

2

LAWNS FROM SOD

ADVANTAGES

Speed With the exception of very large sites, it is possible to lay the sod in just one day.

Ready-to-use The newly laid lawn is able to withstand light traffic almost immediately, and is effectively an "instant" lawn.

No dust and mud The bare earth is completely covered by the turf, which creates a carpet of green; a seeded lawn takes at least several weeks to achieve this goal.

No need for netting Because the grass is already established, it is not prone to attack by birds.

Pest-, disease-, and weed-free Good quality sod should be healthy and weedless.

Flexibility Sod can be laid during periods of the year when seeds will not germinate.

Instant repairs Well-worn areas or damaged patches can be cut out and replaced with a new piece of sod.

DISADVANTAGES

Cost Sod is much more expensive than seed.

Less selection You may not be able to obtain the exact grass varieties that you want.

Effort Stacking, transporting, and laying sods is heavy, back-breaking work and should not be undertaken lightly. However, seeded sod is cut much thinner and rolled, making laying it easier.

Timing Sod must be laid within a day or two of delivery, otherwise the stack must be dismantled and the sods laid out flat if they are not to deteriorate badly.

Variable quality Unless you buy seeded sod, the turf you receive is most likely to be from an agricultural meadow, and will not contain specialist lawn grass varieties. It may also contain a high proportion of weeds, although some sod is treated with selective weed killer before lifting and may be guaranteed weed-free.

PLANNING A LAWN

O nce you have decided you want a new lawn, it is worth spending
a little time on some preliminary planning. Do not be tempted
simply to put down some turf as an instant cover-up for bare earth
or as a quick fix to transform your plot from a building site to
something that looks more like a garden. It makes much better sense
to consider your plans for the garden as a whole, and incorporate
the lawn into those plans right from the start.

2

DESIGN CONSIDERATIONS

The key to ensuring a successful
design is to consider as many options
as possible at the planning stage.

■ **Shape** Choose the outline of the
lawn to fit the overall concept of
your garden. A gently curving lawn
will suit an informally designed
garden better than rigid geometric
shapes, but do not get carried
away: lawns with complex, irregular
shapes are more difficult and time-
consuming to mow and edge.
Equally, a square lawn might be the
best choice for the more geometric
framework of a formal design.

Shrubs screen the shed
from house and patio

Gently curving, irregularly
shaped lawn

Path following sweeping
curves of the lawn

AN INTEGRATED DESIGN
One side of the gently curving
lawn is lined by a hard path,
which provides convenient
and safe access from the
building to the garden shed
and to the gate at the edge of
the property. Using the same
materials for the patio and
path helps to unify the design.

■ **Size** If you have small children, you may want to devote a reasonably large area to the lawn to provide enough space for games and "letting off steam." But if you have set your heart on a highly ornamental, fine quality lawn, it would probably be better to keep the lawn relatively small to reduce maintenance work. Provide an adequate amount of hard surfaced areas such as patios and paths to take the bulk of the foot traffic.

■ **Creating a balance** Do not allow the lawn to be too overwhelming a feature in your garden, with flowerbeds reduced to narrow borders around its edge. Instead, aim for a more balanced mixture of features, perhaps including a patio, borders, raised beds, containers, and a pool.

■ **Position** If one of the main uses of the lawn is to be a play area, site it near the building, where it is easier to keep an eye on children from indoors. If, however, it is to provide a retreat where adults can sit and relax, the lawn may be better sited some distance from the house, perhaps screened by shrubs or hedges.

COPING WITH A SLOPE

A gentle slope makes a perfectly acceptable site for a lawn, but a steeply sloping site presents more of a problem. Grass can be difficult to establish on a gradient, as seedlings tend to be washed down the slope. Once established, a steep slope may also be difficult or dangerous to mow. If the slope is excessive, either move soil from the top to the bottom to reduce the gradient or terrace the site, having two or more areas of level grass with a drop between them. You will need to create mower access to each level, however.

2

DISGUISING A SLOPE
A short flight of steps built into the side of a sloping lawn helps to minimize the gradient.

PREPARING THE SITE

To a large degree, a lawn is only as good as the soil it is growing in. Before you plant the lawn, spend the time and money necessary to dig and amend the soil, creating the best possible environment for the grass. The time you spend at the onset will ultimately save you hours of work struggling to keep an ailing lawn looking presentable.

CLEARING VEGETATION AND STONES

2

The amount of preparatory work involved depends on the conditions you are faced with. You may be replacing an existing, worn-out lawn or converting a flowerbed or shrub border to grass. The site may be overgrown with weeds, or it may be a new plot of (almost) virgin soil.

■ **Removing existing plants** First remove trees and large shrubs, taking out the stumps and as many of the roots as you can. If these are left in the soil they may throw out suckers, encourage fungal growth, or rot, eventually giving rise to dips and hollows in the turf.

Dig up and remove herbaceous plants and weeds; treat perennial weeds and persistent herbaceous plants with a translocated weed killer such as glyphosate to help ensure that small portions of plants and roots left in the soil do not regrow.

■ **Stripping existing turf** Unwanted turf should be stripped off; on a small area this can be done by hand with a sharp spade, but for larger areas a powered turf stripper (which may be rented) makes the job easier.

■ **Clearing rubble** Carefully pick over the soil, removing any large stones, bricks, etc. This is often necessary in the garden plots of new houses, where all sorts of builder's rubble may have been left behind.

CLEARING STONES
Remove all large stones by hand. This process may need to be repeated as more stones are brought to the surface during cultivation.

RAKING OVER
To ensure good germination and rooting use a rake to level the soil and break down large clods before sowing seed or laying sod.

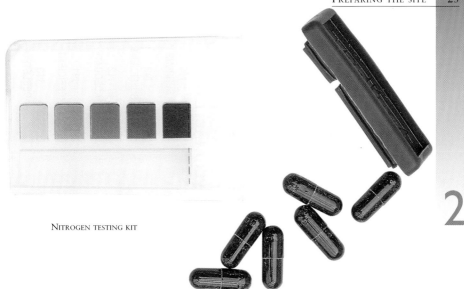

NITROGEN TESTING KIT

2

Once the soil is cleared, it is time to make amends. Grass grown in deep, rich soil will be less vulnerable to pests and diseases. It also should be vigorous enough to choke out weeds.

■ **Test the soil** Before adding soil improvers, send samples to a laboratory for a full report on the pH, nutrient, and content. This information tells you if any fertilizers or amendments need to be added.

■ **Improving soil structure** The best soil amendment is compost. It improves the soil structure of any kind of soil, making clay more friable and sandy soils more bulky. It also adds important microorganisms and microbes to the soil. Of the beneficial microorganisms, some convert nitrogen from the air into water-soluble compounds, making the nutrient available to plants; others interact with plant roots to help them absorb mineral nutrients; and still others feed on harmful plant pathogens. Other amendments include well-rotted manure, which

improves soil texture and fertility, and peat moss, which absorbs and retains a lot of water. Dig in or rototill the amendments to at least 4–6 in (10–15 cm) deep.

DRAINAGE SYSTEMS

If you have a drainage problem where you plan to plant the lawn, deal with it before you plant. Whenever possible, take the simplest solution. Here are two good possibilities:

Swales and drainage ditches
Incorporate swales (a depression or dip that can funnel water) or drainage ditches into your design. You can transform the ditch into a "dry riverbed" by lining it with stones and edging it with moisture-loving plants.

Buried drains Lay tile trains or plastic pipes in 24 in (60 cm) deep trenches. Bed the drains on gravel, then cover with gravel so that water seeps into the drainage channel.

2

DIGGING OVER

Once the site has been cleared, you will need to dig over the soil. For small areas, digging can be done by hand, but for larger lawns it will save time and effort if you rent a powered cultivator. Thoroughly cultivate the site to a depth of 6 in (15 cm) or more, removing any large stones that are brought to the surface. Leave soil in rough clods, allowing these to dry on the surface for a day or two (a spell of sunny, windy weather is ideal), then break them down by treading or striking them with the back of a rake. Tread over the entire site closely to firm the soil.

FINAL SOIL PREPARATIONS

Use a rake to break down the surface of the soil to a fine grade to form a seed bed; without this layer of finely graded soil, germination (and the subsequent lawn) will be patchy and uneven. The soil does not need to be broken down quite so finely for sod, but it should still be firm, level, and well cultivated to encourage the sod to root quickly. Remove clods of soil and large stones, since they will make it more difficult to lay sod and may prevent them from becoming established.

■ **Weed control** By taking an extra four weeks before sowing seed, you can focus on eliminating weeds. After the soil is tilled and smoothed, water regularly until the weed seeds that have been brought to the surface sprout. Uproot them without disturbing the soil surface too much (otherwise you expose yet another crop of weed seeds to the light), or spray with a contact weed killer. This step is unnecessary when laying sod. Weed seeds will not sprout under the thick layer of soil, roots, and grass.

LEVELING THE SURFACE

The next step is to level the surface so that no bumps or hollows remain. For utility lawns, you can do this by eye, moving soil around the surface with a rake, but for a showpiece lawn it is worth using leveling pegs to achieve a perfectly smooth surface.

Bumps and hollows in a lawn make mowing extremely difficult – the high spots will be scalped by the mower blades and the low spots will not be cut properly. Any unevenness in the surface is far more difficult to correct once the lawn is established, so it is worth taking trouble to level the site correctly at the beginning.

■ **Feeding the soil** A few days before sowing seed or laying sod, sprinkle a dressing of a balanced granular or pelleted fertilizer at a rate of 4–6 oz per sq. yd (110–170 g per sq. m) over the surface of the soil and rake it in lightly. Be careful not to upset the level, and try to avoid treading on the prepared soil.

USING FERTILIZER PELLETS
Scatter the fertilizer over the surface of the prepared ground and distribute it evenly around the soil. Rake it in before sowing or laying sod.

MARKING OUT

Wherever possible, the size of the area you prepare should extend beyond the proposed boundaries of the lawn. Use garden canes and string to mark out a geometrically shaped lawn; use a line of sand or a hose laid on the soil surface to mark the rough outline of a curving lawn.

The final shape of the lawn will only be determined once you have cut the edges of the established grass, so at this stage you need to make the lawn slightly larger than its eventual desired size.

USING LEVELING PEGS

CREATING A LEVEL SURFACE
First make sure that the prepared soil is well firmed by treading down the whole area thoroughly.

• With a marker pen, draw a line on each leveling peg at the same distance from the top.

• Use a straight edge to place the first line of pegs, then knock subsequent lines of pegs into the ground in a grid formation across the site, inserting rows of pegs at about 3 ft (1 m) intervals. Check with a spirit level to make sure that the tops of the pegs are level.

• Adjust the soil with a rake so that it is level with the marks on each of the pegs. Remove the pegs before laying the sod or sowing seed.

CREATING A SLOPING LAWN
• Starting at the top of the proposed site, mark the pegs for each row at an increasingly lower level. The difference in level between each row should be minimal, to achieve a gentle gradient.

1 Dig over the soil, removing large stones and weeds. Fertilize if necessary, then firm the surface.

2 Mark out the straight edges of the new lawn with canes and string, pulling the string taut.

3 Use a line of sand to mark out the shape of any curved edges. This can be worked into the soil later.

2

SOWING SEED

W arm-season grass seed sprouts and establishes best when it
is planted in late spring or early summer at a temperature of
between 70°F and 90°F (21°C and 32°C). Cool-season turf grasses do
best when sown in late summer or early fall when the weather is
cooling and fall rains will keep them moist. They also sprout well in
early- to mid-spring, but you usually need to supplement rainfall with
additional irrigation until they are well established. Spring-sown cool-
season grasses are prone to weeds that are sprouting at the same time.

WHEN TO SOW

One of the advantages of growing a
lawn from seed rather than laying
turf grass sod is that it is possible to
choose the most suitable day for
sowing. The seed will not spoil as
sod will if you have to wait a few
days for the weather to improve. The
soil should be moist, but dry enough
to walk on comfortably. Sprinkle it
lightly before you sow if the soil is
dry. Choose a calm, still day,
especially if you are hand-sowing;
it is very difficult to achieve even
coverage if the seed is being blown
about as you broadcast it. Ideally the
weather on the day of sowing should
be dry with light rain forecast within
the next few days. If rain does not
fall, keep the seeds continually moist
with a fine sprinkler spray.

CHOOSING THE SOWING RATE

THICK SOWING

• A high sowing rate allows for losses
resulting from seed being eaten by
birds and low germination rates due
to poor soil conditions or the use of
inferior grass varieties.

• Thick sowing gives an increased
density of seedlings, resulting in
quicker grass coverage.

• Thickly sown grass seedlings are
better able to compete with weeds,
which may soon colonize bare soil
in thinly sown areas.

• Thick sowing results in reduced
moisture loss from bare soil, making
seedlings less prone to damage from
high temperatures in summer.

THIN SOWING

• A low sowing rate uses less seed
overall, so is more economical.

• In the long term, thinly sown
seedlings have a better chance of
growing into strong plants, since they
receive relatively more food, light, and
air than thickly sown seedlings.

• Thinly sown seedlings are less likely
to suffer from a problem known as
"damping off." This is caused by fungi
that thrive in the humid conditions
that arise in heavily seeded areas.

SOWING RATE

Measure the total area of the proposed lawn to work out how much seed you need to buy. Lawn seed is sold by weight; the weight of individual seeds varies markedly between the different species and varieties, and this, together with the fact that some species germinate more reliably than others, leads to differences in the recommended application rates. For professional seeding of large areas of grass, sowing rates can vary between ⅛ and 1½ oz per sq. yd (5 g and 50 g per sq. m). For domestic purposes, however, the rate is less critical; grass seed is generally sown at around 1–1½ oz per sq. yd (35–50 g per sq. m) to give a good, dense cover. Always check the supplier's recommended sowing rate for the seed mix you buy. Prepacked seed will give the dimensions of the area it will cover on each packet of seed.

2

1 Weigh out into a pot half the recommended amount of seed to cover 1 sq. yd (1 sq. m). Ensure no seed escapes from the bottom of the pot.

2 Draw a line on the side of the pot to mark the level of seed required, and use this as a guide when calculating subsequent batches.

3 Measure and mark out a square plot, using canes laid on the soil surface. Broadcast the seed from side to side, then sow another batch, this time at right angles to the first.

Warning

Grass seed is often extremely dusty. To avoid breathing in the dust, always wear a mask when sowing.

HOW TO SOW A LAWN

O n a still day you can broadcast seed evenly in a small area by
flinging handfuls of seed off your fingertips. For more accurate
distribution, use a drop-type or rotary spreader, or broadcast spreader
both of which can be rented. The drop-type spreader is more precise in
its distribution. Overlap the strips slightly to avoid missing a section.

SOWING STEP BY STEP

2

1 Choose a dry,
preferably windless
day for sowing. Give the
soil a final light raking if
necessary to ensure that
it is broken down into
fine crumbs and that the
surface is even.

2 Using canes or string, divide the
area to be sown into plots
measuring 1 sq. yd (1 sq. m). Measure
out batches of seed (see p. 29) and
broadcast it evenly from side to side
over each plot in turn, until you have
covered the whole area.

3 Lightly rake over the area to settle the seeds into the soil surface but do not try to bury the seeds, since this may prevent good germination.

2

4 Water the seeds with a fine spray, being careful not to dislodge them from their resting place or to flood the area so they begin to run off. Deter birds by covering the newly sown seed with a floating row cover or mulch lightly with weed-free hay. The seeds must be kept continually moist until they sprout.

TIP

On reasonably small lawns you can mark out the entire area in evenly sized squares and sow each square as shown in Step 2. On larger lawns it is quicker to use one square as an example to show what the correct coverage looks like, then sow the rest of the lawn by eye, referring back to the original square occasionally to ensure the coverage remains consistent.

MARKING OUT WITH CANES

LAYING SOD

Sod is pre-grown grass that is stripped off the ground and sold in rolls or folded. In most cases, the grass is grown over the winter and harvested the following year. Some states have sod certification programs that guarantee established standards of quality. Before you buy, make sure that the grasses are suitable for your purposes.

CHOOSING SOD

2

The best-quality sod generally is grown by professional producers who take part in state inspection programs. These schemes require growers to meet their standards for prescribed varieties and mixtures as well as undergo preplanting, mid-production, and final preharvest inspections. Sod grown in this program that does not meet the high standards may be sold as "approved" rather than "certified" sod, and sold at a lower price. High-quality sod is available outside state certification programs, but it may not be graded by uniform standards.

STACKING TURF GRASS SOD

Generally sod is delivered rolled or folded. The carpetlike strips are up to 1 in (2.5 cm) thick, 12 in (30 cm) wide, and about 6 ft (1.8 m) long. Each strip can cover about 10 sq. ft (0.9 sq. m). When you receive your delivery:

• Have the pallets placed in a shady spot near the area you want to cover.

• Examine the sod and reject any pieces with rips or holes or that show signs of pests or disease.

• Lay the sod within 48 hours of delivery. If you cannot begin work right away, unroll the strips and lay them flat. Be sure to keep them moist. If you need to stack the sod, put no more than three or four strips in a stack. They can be left like that for up to 24 hours in cold weather and no more than 12 hours on hot days.

TURF PYRAMID

WATERING TURF

■ **What to look for** Whatever sod you buy, make sure that it has been freshly harvested. Look for a moist, green mat with plenty of healthy roots that do not form a tight mass. If the grass is tall and the mat has a tight tangle of roots, it was probably harvested some time ago and you should reject it. Also reject any sod with yellowing blades of grass. The yellow indicates either that the sod was harvested several days ago and left rolled up, or that it is suffering from disease.

■ **When to lay sod** You can lay sod at any time of year when the grass is actively growing. Early summer is ideal for warm-season grasses; spring or fall is best for cool-season species. Summer also works for both warm- and cool-season varieties, however you must be prepared to water the new lawn much more often to keep the grass and the soil underneath properly moist.

■ **Calculating quantities** Work out the size of the area you plan to sod, and then add at least an extra 5% to allow for waste and shaping. If the space is not a simple rectangle, divide the area into quadrants (with a semicircle or circle if necessary). Calculate the area of each space, and then add the numbers together to arrive at a total quantity.

PREPARING THE SITE

For areas where the new lawn does not abut against an edging, mark out the boundaries before you begin laying the sod. A string stretched between two pegs or stakes hammered in the ground is an easy way to delineate a straight edge. For curving lines, lay down a piece of hose and experiment with different curves until you find the one most pleasing to you. You can either leave the hose in that position until the sod is laid and cut to shape, or hammer in stakes along the edge to mark it. If you have already tilled the soil for planting, be careful not to walk on it too much, compacting it.

When laying sod, your goal is to encourage the roots to penetrate into the native soil as quickly as possible to anchor it and allow it to become well established. To encourage the roots of sod to grow downward, you need moist, nutrient-rich soil. Prepare the soil for sod as you would for sowing seed (see pp. 25–26), amending to improve the soil structure and fertility, grading and leveling, and then raking to provide a smooth bed. Water the soil well before you lay the sod so the roots make immediate contact with a moist surface.

AVOIDING SOIL COMPACTION
Use wooden planks to avoid having to walk on the prepared surface. This will help to spread your weight and avoid compacting the soil.

HOW TO LAY SOD

A rrange for sod to be delivered on the day you plan to lay it. If left stacked for even a few hours in the sun, the sod can be damaged. Laying sod is hard and heavy work, but you have the immediate satisfaction of seeing an expanse of bare earth being transformed into a verdant lawn before your eyes.

LAYING SOD

2

1 First moisten the ground so that the top layer is well watered but not soggy. Begin laying full strips of sod along one side – ideally against a straight edge – of the area you plan to cover. Use full strips of sod along the perimeter; thin strips dry out more quickly than wide ones and should be used in the center. Keep the joints as tight as possible without overlapping or stretching the pieces. Work from the sodded area to open soil.

2 Avoid using cut off pieces of sod at the end of a row; it will be vulnerable to drying out. Use the short pieces in the middle of rows. To join two pieces at an odd angle, lay one piece over the other and cut through both pieces with a knife. Remove the underneath scrap piece and firm down the top section into the joint. Tamp down the completed rows to ensure good soil contact.

2

3 Continue laying each row, staggering the joints like bricks. To protect the fragile grass, lay a board or plank across where you need to walk or kneel. Do not walk directly on the prepared soil or the laid sod strips. Always lay the sod strips in straight lines, even if the final lawn is to be curved. Let straight strips overlap the edges of curves, and then cut them to shape when you have finished.

4 Sod should be deeply watered within half an hour of being laid. Set up the sprinkler to water one section while you continue to work on the next. The water should penetrate at least 6 in (15 cm) to encourage a deep root system. Water the sod daily for two to three weeks after laying, making sure the water penetrates deeply. The deeper you water, the more drought-tolerant the lawn.

CARE OF NEW LAWNS

L awns need special care in their first few months, particularly
a lawn sown from seed. This is a vital period in establishing a
strong-growing, healthy lawn that will look good and wear well.
Sufficient moisture is probably the most essential element in
promoting good root growth early on and to prevent the delicate
seedlings or newly laid turf from drying out.

LAWNS FROM SEED

2

■ **Watering** Seeds and young sprouts
need to be kept continually moist to
grow. Whenever the ground starts to
dry, sprinkle the area gently to avoid
washing the seeds or seedlings away.
In hot, dry weather you may need to
water as often as two to four times a
day. Aim to keep the seed bed moist
to a depth of 1–2 in (2.5–5 cm).
As the seedlings grow, reduce the
frequency of watering, but increase
the depth the water soaks in to
encourage deep roots. Plugs and
sprigs also need to be kept moist,

but you should avoid waterlogging
the ground. The plants may not take
root if the soil is too wet.

■ **The first cut** Do not mow until the
shoots are firmly rooted. Wait until
they reach 3–4 in (8–10 cm) to cut
the grass for the first time. A reel
mower is best for cutting young grass
because it is less likely to uproot the
fragile shoots. If you have a rotary
mower, make sure the blade is very
sharp, and set the throttle to slow.
Even for species that can take a close
shave, set the mower to cut 3 in
(8 cm) high for the first two or three
mowings. Mow sprigs and plugs
once they are well rooted, to
encourage them to spread and fill in.

ROLLER

■ **Regular mowing** Ideally you
should remove up to one-third of
the shoot growth at any one time;
cutting any more than this will check
the lawn's development. While most
homeowners settle into a weekly
routine of mowing during periods
of fast growth, particularly in early
spring, you may need to do the job
more often. Leave the cut clippings
on the lawn to return important
nutrients to the grass.

■ **Using the lawn** Once the lawn has
been mown several times, it can take
light traffic but should be walked on
as little as possible for the first year.

LAWNS FROM SOD

■ **Watering** Like a seedbed, turf grass sod needs to be kept continually moist. If there is no rain, water daily, making sure the water penetrates through the layer of turf to the soil beneath.

■ **The first cut** After laying sod, wait until the grass is growing vigorously, about three weeks, before mowing for the first time. Check that the sod has rooted by tugging gently on a corner. You should feel resistance. As an extra precaution against accidentally lifting up a strip of sod with your mower, the first few times you mow run the machine perpendicular to the direction the strips are laid. If you are using a rotary mower, set the throttle to slow to reduce the pulling on the grass.

■ **Using the lawn** Sod lawns can take light traffic fairly soon after laying, but avoid heavy traffic until the lawn is well established.

■ **Fertilizing** Wait at least six weeks before you fertilize. Opt for a light application of nitrogen. After that, follow normal fertilization practices as recommended (see pp. 70–73).

2

WATERING TURF
It is essential to keep a new lawn well watered. If sod or seedlings are allowed to dry out, you will be left with ugly bare or brown patches.

MAKING THE FIRST CUT
The first cut should barely tip the new blades of grass. If the shoots are reduced by too much, the grass may take a long time to recover.

TROUBLESHOOTING

A number of problems may emerge early on with both seed-sown and sod lawns. Examine the lawn every day to make sure that it gets off to a good start. If the grass does not appear to be thriving, you must be prepared to act quickly to remedy the problem.

SEED-SOWN LAWNS

2

■ **Seedlings fail to appear** The seeds may not have germinated at all, or if they did, the may have failed to develop. There are several possible causes: the use of poor quality, old seed; an insufficient supply of moisture; burying the seeds too deeply; or a "cap" or hard crust on the soil surface may have prevented the seedlings from breaking through.

■ **Patchy germination** The prime cause is uneven sowing, but inadequately cultivated soil and poor-quality seed could also be to blame. Damage by birds, cats, or dogs is another possible cause.

■ **Yellow, dying grass** Drought is usually the cause of this problem and is best avoided by watering the new lawn gently but thoroughly as often as necessary in dry weather. Fungus diseases (see pp. 95–96) may also develop, especially in shady areas or where air circulation is poor. Excessive wear and damage by pets or other animals also may kill off the grass.

■ **Weeds overrun newly sown grass** To prevent a flush of weeds in a newly sown lawn, leave the proposed site fallow for three to four weeks after preparing the soil and allow weeds to sprout. Then either rake the weeds off or treat them with a contact weed killer. Alternatively, sow the grass seed a little more thickly than recommended to enable it to compete effectively with weeds. If necessary use a lawn weed killer especially formulated for new lawns.

SOD LAWNS

■ **Sod shrinks, leaving gaps** Make sure you abut the sod strips closely when laying them. Brush top-dressing into the cracks between each strip and water the newly laid lawn daily, especially in dry or windy weather.

DYING GRASS
Long strips of a newly laid lawn have already turned yellow, probably because of lack of rain. The grass will die if not watered very soon.

Restoring an existing lawn

Assessing lawn quality 40
Describes points to watch for when deciding whether a lawn
can be repaired, and common causes of damage

Underlying problems 42
Examines how soil, weather, and shade can all adversely
affect the quality of your lawn

Preliminary work 44
Looks at the work you will have to do before beginning your
lawn restoration program

Making improvements 46
Offers a year-round guide to lawn improvement, with clear details of
what to do in each season

Lawn repairs 48
Describes how to carry out simple reseeding or returfing
of bare or damaged patches, and ragged edges

3

RESTORING AN EXISTING LAWN

When you are faced with a tired, worn out piece of grass masquerading as a lawn, it is often difficult to know just how to go about restoring it to something that is more worthy of the name. In cases where the damage is extreme, the only option may be to start again from scratch by digging up the area, but often it is possible to work with what you have, improving the existing lawn through remedial actions and better cultivation practices. Often if you remove all thatch from the grass, aerate it, overseed to fill in gaps, and fertilize with organic fertilizer, your lawn will rejuvenate into a beautiful green sward.

3

The best time of year to renovate cool-season grasses is in spring or early fall when the cooler weather and more frequent rains will promote new growth. Warm-season grasses begin their most active growth during late spring when the weather begins to warm up. Start working on them at that time of year to allow the root system to re-establish itself before winter's cooler weather. Because most of the species spread by aboveground stolons or rhizomes, the warm-season grasses are particularly prone to thatch.

Assessing lawn quality

B y neglecting a lawn for too long, or simply giving it the wrong treatment, its condition will deteriorate very quickly. You may inherit a poor quality lawn when you move house, or perhaps you have been guilty of neglecting the garden yourself. Before you set about restoring a lawn to good order, first assess the scale of the problem.

What to look for

■ **Thatch buildup** If a dense, interwoven mat of stolons, stems, rhizomes, and leaf blades forms on the soil surface, water and nutrients cannot penetrate, and the lawn suffers.

■ **Compacted soil** If the lawn receives heavy traffic, especially when it is wet, the soil will compact, blocking the flow of water and oxygen to the plants.

■ **Weed infestation** The lawn may be colonized by broad-leaved weeds and moss.

Mistreatment

■ **Irregular mowing** When the grass becomes too long, you might be tempted to cut it back to the appropriate length all at once. However, if you remove more than one-third of the grass's length at one time, you will give the lawn a severe shock that sets back its vigor. The grass will perform better if you reduce the height gradually across several mowings.

DECORATIVE PATHS
A series of intertwining tile pathways provides an ingenious and decorative way of preventing worn areas on a small circular lawn.

■ **Mowing too closely** A lawn that is mown too short will grow faster in an attempt to replace the lost leaf blades, actually increasing the frequency that you need to mow. Eventually all that effort put into growing will weaken the grass. Grass left longer grows more slowly, blocks out weeds, and withstands drought better.

■ **Misuse of fertilizers** Applying fertilizers unevenly or at the wrong rates, so that some areas receive a double dose, can seriously weaken or even kill patches of grass. The time of year also is an important consideration when fertilizing: applying a nitrogen-rich spring fertilizer to a lawn in the fall will encourage lush, soft growth that may be damaged by winter cold.

■ **Excessive foot traffic** Heavy pedestrian traffic, especially when the grass is wet, will compact the soil and wear away areas of grass, creating bald patches.

RESTORE OR REPLACE?

If there is a reasonable proportion of good quality turf grass still present over most of the lawn area, it is possible to carry out an improvement program that gradually will restore the lawn to good condition over several seasons. Deciding whether to renovate or replace a poor-quality lawn often comes down to how quickly you want results – the process of renovation could take many years. However, if a large proportion of the lawn has some or all of the problems listed above, it is unlikely ever to be restored to a satisfactory state. In such cases, it is better to strip off what remains of the turf and start again with a new lawn as described in Chapter 2.

GROWING TREES IN A LAWN
If tree roots break through the lawn surface, remove a circle of sod to the extent of the exposed roots and cover the soil with gravel.

3

COMMON PROBLEMS

Below is a checklist of the problems you are most likely to encounter when renovating a lawn. Advice on how to identify and deal with these problems is given on pages 84–102.
• Weed and moss infestation
• Pest damage
• Worn pathways or other areas
• Uneven lawn surface
• Waterlogging/drainage problems
• Frost, snow, and wind damage
• Damage caused by incorrect mowing
• Scorching caused by over-fertilization
• Inadequate watering
• Insufficient light
• Turf diseases

STEPPINGSTONE SUITABLE FOR AREAS OF HEAVY TRAFFIC

UNDERLYING PROBLEMS

A poor-quality lawn may be the result not just of neglect but of more serious problems to do with the site and underlying growing conditions. Problems of this nature may be difficult or impossible to correct, in which case you should consider some other form of ground cover or hard landscaping to replace the lawn; often, however, you can improve conditions to make a lawn a more viable proposition.

3

POOR TOPSOIL

The ideal soil for a lawn is a fertile, free-draining loam, but few gardens are blessed with perfect soil. Heavy soils containing a high proportion of clay may need to be lightened by the addition of sand, which will improve the drainage, but in severe cases you will need to install a drainage system to prevent waterlogging (see p. 25). Very sandy soils, on the other hand, may drain too freely, washing plant nutrients away with the water; the incorporation of bulky organic matter such as garden compost or well-rotted manure will help here.

POOR SUBSOIL

The soil in the gardens of new houses often consists of a very thin layer of topsoil over infertile subsoil; it may also contain a large quantity of builders' rubble. In these cases you will need to import a reasonable depth of new topsoil.

First improve the structure of the subsoil by digging it thoroughly, removing large stones and the roots of perennial weeds at the same time. Then cover the subsoil with at least 12 in (30 cm) of good quality topsoil, taking care not to mix it with the subsoil beneath.

ANALYZING YOUR SOIL

If you are not sure of the type of soil in your garden, take some soil samples and have them analyzed professionally. Take soil from several areas of the site to get a good overall picture. Lawns grow best on fertile, free-draining loam that is neutral or slightly acid. Home-testing kits are also available but a professional test will give a more detailed analysis.

The test results give information about the relative proportions of clay, sand, peat, chalk, and silt in the soil, as well as indicating its nutrient levels and degree of acidity (pH).

CLAY SOIL

WEATHER EXTREMES

If your area is prone to extremes of temperature, heavy rainfall, or drought, use grass species that are most tolerant of the prevailing conditions or install good drainage or irrigation systems.

■ **High temperatures** Hot weather is usually accompanied by drought; a well-established lawn can survive quite severe drought (although it will lose its green color if not watered) but the adverse conditions allow weeds and coarse grasses to flourish.

■ **Low temperatures** Cool-season grasses are fairly tolerant of low temperatures but are still prone to physical damage in cold weather: for example, by walking over frosty turf you may kill the grass.

GREEN SHADE
Some trees, such as this willow, can cast deep shade over much of the lawn. A shade-resistant grass seed mixture is essential in such cases.

SHADE

Shade cast on a lawn is a common problem, since most grass species do not thrive in shady conditions. The shade may come from adjacent buildings or overhanging trees. Shade cast by trees is a particularly difficult problem, as the trees' roots also compete with the grass for moisture and nutrients. "Green" shade also alters the quality as well as quantity of light that the grass receives.

Shade affects temperature as well as light; shady areas are cooler than those in full sun, and have a higher level of humidity, encouraging fungal diseases and moss in the grass.

Shade caused by trees may be improved by removing the lower branches of the trees or, of course, by removing the trees altogether to allow more light to penetrate.

Some species of grass are far more tolerant of shade than others so, where appropriate, use seed mixtures that are adapted to coping with shady conditions (see p. 102).

3

PRELIMINARY WORK

If your neglected lawn has been moderately well (if sometimes incorrectly) cared for, you will probably be able to start on the improvement program outlined on pages 46–47 straight away. However, you may be faced with a lawn that has been seriously neglected for some time, in which case you have a major restoration job to tackle. Spring is by far the best time to start.

HOW TO BEGIN

■ **Do a rough cut** On a neglected lawn, the grass and weeds will be tall and overgrown, so the first job is to cut them down to about 4 in (10 cm) high. You may use a scythe for this job, but a motorized alternative such as a brushcutter is quicker and usually safer. This equipment can be rented if needed. Before you start, walk over the site and remove large stones and other obstructions that may be difficult to see.

■ **Remove debris** Once the grass has been cut to a more workable height, remove any stones and garbage from

the site. Remove any unwanted shrubs in the lawn.

■ **Mow** Set the blades on your lawn mower as high as possible so that no more than one-third of the height of the grass is removed. Over several mowings, gradually reduce the lawn to the desired height.

■ **Re-assess the lawn** Cut out and examine a small cross-section of the lawn. If the layer of thatch is more than 1 in (2.5cm) thick and if the soil is highly compacted, you will need to dethatch and aerate.

REMOVING DEBRIS
Rake over the ground to remove debris such as stones and builders' rubble before making the first cut with a lawn mower.

REPLACING GRASS
For children's play areas and well-used paths replace grass with more resilient materials such as wood chips, gravel, or paving.

■ **Plan paths and hard surfaces**
Identify areas of heavy traffic and
make adjustments to the layout of
the lawn, if necessary. A frequently
used route (between the house door
and garden gate, for example)
may need to be turned into a firm-
surfaced path; children's play areas
could be resurfaced with wood chips,
and so on. It may be possible to
redirect traffic around the lawn and
on to adjacent pathways. Avoid
making these routes too circuitous,

otherwise, even with the best of
intentions, they will not be used.

■ **Repair damaged areas** Reseed
thin or worn patches. Choose a seed
mix that is close to the grass in your
existing lawn so you make a good
match of color and blade texture.
If you have no idea what grasses
comprise your lawn, overseed the
entire area for a consistent, even
result. Choose a grass mix that
suits your situation and needs.

OVERSOWING WORN AREAS

If you know roughly what grasses are
in your lawn, you can reseed with
the same type of grasses, saving the

work and expense of oversowing the
entire lawn. Keep newly seeded areas
moist until the seeds germinate.

3

1 Rake the area to scratch up the soil
surface slightly and to remove any
dead plant material so the seeds can
make good contact with the soil.

2 Unless it is a very large area, it will
be quicker to handsow the seed,
rather than use a spreader. Sprinkle
an even layer of seed over the area.

SETTING OBJECTIVES

As well as performing any necessary
preparatory work, now is the time to
start making plans to carry out lawn
maintenance on a regular basis (see
Chapter 4). This advance planning will
ensure that your objectives for the
lawn are achieved and maintained.
Your key objectives for your lawn
should be to:

• Improve the health, vigor, and
appearance of the existing grass;

• Encourage the growth of desirable
grass species rather than weeds;

• Produce a lawn with a strong
growth that will be able to shrug
off occasional heavy wear, drought,
or other stresses.

MAKING IMPROVEMENTS

A shabby, poor-quality lawn cannot be transformed overnight, but a continuing program of correct care will soon begin to show results. The following steps summarize the techniques that you will need to carry out regularly during each season, beginning in spring, which is the best time to start an improvement program. More details on all the techniques mentioned below can be found in Chapter 4.

SPRING

■ **Mow** Start mowing the grass as soon as it begins growing in spring. Ideally you should mow as often as necessary so you remove only one-third of the blade at any one time. When the grass is growing quickly, that may be as often as twice a week. If you are cutting off just the recommended one-third of the grass blade, leave the clippings on the lawn. If the grass is too long, bag the clippings or rake them up after mowing. The clippings make excellent mulch or compost.

■ **Trim edges and make repairs** If the edges of the lawn have been neglected, recut them with a sharp edging iron (see p. 62); use a plank and taut string for precision when cutting straight edges and a hose or rope to mark out any curves. Repair damaged edges and bare patches (see pp. 48–52). Trim the recut edges with long-handled shears or a powered trimmer after mowing.

■ **Apply a fertilizer** To build your soil as well as feed your lawn, use an organic fertilizer. Grass fertilizers for spring contain a high proportion of nitrogen to stimulate active growth.

SUMMER

■ **Control weeds** A selective lawn weed killer will kill broad-leaved weeds without damaging the grass. Avoid the most controversial chemicals, such as 2,4-D. Also consider less toxic choices for weed control such as applying lime to discourage weeds, such as sorrels and mosses, that prefer acid soil.

■ **Continue to mow** Keep the lawn at the length suitable for your grass type (see p. 60), cutting off no more than one-third of the grass at any mowing.

■ **Water** Encourage a deep root system by irrigating so the water penetrates the soil to a depth of at least 6 in (15 cm).

COLLECTING GRASS CLIPPINGS
Collect the grass cuttings only if the grass is so long that the clippings clump together. Otherwise leave the cuttings on the lawn.

FALL AND WINTER

■ **Dethatching** In early fall, scarify the lawn if the thatch is thicker than 1 in (2.5 cm). Use a handheld spring-tined rake for small lawns or a powered dethatcher for larger projects.

■ **Aerate the soil** A garden fork poked into the ground at frequent intervals and at varying angles will do a good job of introducing oxygen into the soil. For small lawns a garden fork or pronged shoes are adequate to do the job. For large spaces, rent an aerating machine that lifts out the cores of soil (see pp. 74–75).

■ **Top-dressing** Incorporate organic material into soil by top dressing with 1 cu. yd (0.7 cu. m) of compost per 1,000 sq. ft (90 sq. m) of lawn before aerating. On thin or patchy lawns,

mix grass seed with top dressing and keep moist until the seeds germinate.

■ **Apply a fall feed** Fall is the most important time to feed cool-season lawns, keeping the grass growing into the cold weather, and giving it the reserves it needs until spring. Feed warm-season grasses in late summer.

■ **Raking** Keep fallen leaves raked up regularly or they will smother the grass. Use the raked leaves for mulch in borders or add them to the compost pile.

■ **Prepare the mower for winter** Drain gas from the tank on the mower, clean and oil equipment, and sharpen mower blades so that they are ready for spring.

3

AERATING THE SOIL
Working methodically across the lawn, insert a garden fork to a depth of 4 in (10 cm), each time moving the fork gently forward and back.

FLY MOWER
The fly or hover mower, designed to float on a cushion of air and cut with a rotary blade, is useful for mowing steep slopes.

LAWN REPAIRS

B are patches and ragged edges are a common problem in neglected lawns. Even on the best-kept lawns there are bound to be isolated incidents when accidents or pests damage the turf. But do not despair; such damage can usually be successfully remedied so that the repair becomes invisible within a matter of weeks.

RESEEDING AND RETURFING

There are two options for repairing damaged patches of lawn: reseeding and returfing.

■ **Blending in repairs** Choose a seed mix that approximates what is already in your lawn, or patch with a piece of sod from another part of your lawn so that the new grass blends in with the surrounding turf.

■ **Reseeding a patch** When repairing a lawn by reseeding, the seed mixture should match exactly the mixture used for the rest of the lawn. When sowing a new lawn, always keep a note of the seed mixture you use, including details of the varieties and their proportions. If you do not know which grass varieties were used in the lawn, read the descriptions on a variety of seed bags and select a mixture that seems to offer the closest match.

When reseeding an area of lawn, spread the seed mixture beyond the bare patch and into the existing grass. This will effectively blur the edges of the resown patch, disguising it more successfully.

RESEEDING A BARE PATCH

Mid- to late spring and early fall are the best times to carry out reseeding repairs. Reseeding may also be done in summer, if necessary, but you need to take special care to keep the soil moist in periods of hot, dry weather.

1 Dig over the soil in the bare patch, removing any weeds. Rake over the soil, then lightly firm the surface by tamping it down with a rake.

2 Sow grass seed evenly at a rate of 1½ oz per sq. yd (50 g per sq. m) and rake it in gently. Cover the whole area with a thin layer of sifted soil.

3

USING GERMINATED LAWN SEED

You may get more reliable results when reseeding damaged areas of lawn if you use pregerminated seed.

The reseeded areas are easier to identify with this method, since the new shoots are visible straight away.

3

1 Use a watering can and rose to lightly moisten a bucket of sowing compost. Add the water gradually to avoid making the compost too wet.

2 Sprinkle some grass seed on to the moist compost and combine the mixture gently but thoroughly by stirring it with a trowel.

3 Transfer small quantities of the mixture to seed boxes or plant pots, leaving it for two days until germination has begun.

4 When the seeds have begun to germinate spread the mixture over the prepared bare patch, pressing it gently into the soil with your fingers.

AFTER CARE

If the weather is dry, use a watering can with a fine rose attachment to water the resown area. Cover the repair with a piece of horticultural fabric to help keep moisture in the soil and protect the seed from birds.

Mark the repair with canes and string to deter foot traffic and pets until the seedlings are established. When the newly sown grass is growing strongly, begin mowing the area at the same time as the rest of the lawn.

RETURFING A BARE PATCH

The best season for returfing is early fall, although spring is also a suitable time. Avoid returfing in summer, since the new sod is likely to dry out and shrink, causing gaps to appear around the edges of the repair.

3

1 Measure the bare patch then use a sharp knife to cut a piece of fresh sod that is 10–15 percent bigger than required to ensure complete coverage. Place the new sod lightly in position over the damaged patch.

2 Using a sharp edging iron, cut around the edge of the new sod and into the lawn below. Put the replacement sod to one side, then use a sharp spade to lift the cut section of damaged sod cleanly.

3 Break up the soil beneath the damaged section with a hand fork, then firm it down well with the back of a rake. If necessary, make small adjustments to the level of the soil so that the replacement sod will lie flush with the lawn surface.

4 Place the new sod in position, firming it down well with the back of a rake to make sure that there is good soil contact across the entire area. Top-dress the joints with a mixture of equal parts peat (or peat substitute) and sand, then water well.

BUMPS AND HOLLOWS

An even surface for a lawn is a necessity and not just for the sake of appearance. Small bumps and hollows make the lawn difficult to mow and may make it awkward to walk over without stumbling or tripping. Hollows in a lawn tend to hold moisture, so the grass growing in them is lusher and more prone to disease; bumps are prone to drying out and are scalped by mower blades, often becoming bare.

3

1 Use a sharp knife to cut through the bump or hollow, making either a cross or an "H" shape through the turf. Center the cut on the irregularity, extending it slightly beyond the area.

2 Carefully peel back the flaps of sod to expose the soil. Do this gently to avoid making unsightly tears or cracks in the lawn. Extend the cuts to ease lifting the flaps, if necessary.

3 Remove soil from a bump or add soil to a hollow, as necessary, until the area is level with the surrounding soil. Firm the soil surface down by treading it with your foot.

4 Fold back the sod, tamping it down well to ensure good contact with the soil beneath. Top-dress with equal parts peat and sand, working it into the joints, and water thoroughly.

RAGGED EDGES

Lawn edges are particularly prone to damage especially on light, crumbly soils. Foot traffic and the use of wheelbarrows on adjacent pathways may cause small areas of minor damage. More extensive sections of lawn edging may become ragged as a result of overhanging plants from a flowerbed. Fortunately, ragged edges are relatively easy to repair.

3

1 Use a sharp edging iron and a straight edge (such as a piece of timber) to cut out a straight-sided section of sod around the damaged edge. Undercut the section carefully with a spade.

2 Slide the undercut sod forward until the damaged portion extends beyond the lawn edge. Using a piece of wood as a straight edge, trim off the damaged piece so that the new edge is flush with the rest of the lawn.

3 Cut a replacement piece of sod to fit the gap that has been formed. Fork over the exposed soil lightly and firm it well, then place the new piece of turf in position, ensuring that it is in firm contact with the soil. Top-dress the whole repair, working the top-dressing well into the joints.

ALTERNATIVE STEP

If the edge is only a little ragged, follow Step 1 but then lift the sod and turn it round so that the ragged edge lies toward the center of the lawn. Firm the sod and sprinkle the bare patch with sifted topsoil and grass seed. Water well.

Lawn maintenance

Choosing a mower 54
Outlines reasons for mowing, and describes how to choose a mower

Types of mower 58
Looks at the different mowing actions of lawn mowers

Mowing 60
Explains how to mow, how to calculate the right height of cut,
and what to do with grass clippings

Tools and equipment 62
Outlines essential tools and pieces of equipment, and optional extras

Edging and trimming 64
Describes how to keep lawn edges looking good through
careful choice of lawn shape, and good tool-buying decisions

Watering 66
Examines why lawns need water, and how to be sure
your lawn gets the right amount of water

Watering methods 68
Outlines the advantages and disadvantages of hand watering, and
using hoses, sprinklers, and timer devices

Using fertilizers 70
Explains why lawns need feeding, and how to devise a feeding program

Applying fertilizers 72
Describes how to fertilize your lawn, and outlines the differences
between slow- and fast-release fertilizers

Soil aeration 74
Looks at the why and how of lawn aeration

Dethatching 76
Explains thatch buildup and how to remedy the problem

Weeds and diseases 78
Outlines how to eliminate weeds and diseases

4

LAWN MAINTENANCE

The key to keeping a lawn looking good is to give it regular attention, rather than waiting until something goes wrong before taking action. Although lawns need consistent care, especially throughout the growing season, the work involved need not be too time consuming. Mowing, edging, feeding, watering, and weed control are the basic routine tasks.

You can avoid problems of weeds, pests, and diseases if you provide your lawn with a good environment where the grass can flourish as a vigorous, healthy plant. In this chapter you will learn how to manage the care of your lawn so that it can be as healthy as possible without overfeeding, overwatering, or overmowing. You will save money and with luck you will be rewarded with some spare time to relax and enjoy the beautiful swath of green that you have created.

4

CHOOSING A MOWER

In the days before the advent of the lawn mower, the turf in parkland that was attached to the stately homes and mansions of wealthy families was kept short by teams of men with scythes, or by large flocks of sheep. The invention of the reel machine in 1830 allowed a close-clipped lawn to become a feature of everyone's garden.

THE PURPOSE OF MOWING

Grass is mowed for a number of reasons, principally to improve its appearance and maintain a practical surface for walking on or playing games. Mowing also improves the quality of the lawn by keeping broad-leaved weeds under control and stimulating the growth of new grass shoots. The grass is able to withstand regular cutting because the leaves regenerate from the base of the plant.

A PLEA FOR TALLER GRASS

When you cut the grass, you are forcing it to survive at a lower height than it would in the wild. Too-close mowing eventually weakens the lawn, making it more susceptible to drought and extreme cold. In contrast, taller grass has more leaf area for photosynthesis, making it more vigorous and disease-resistant. A longer lawn will also block out light that weeds such as crabgrass, purslane, and chickweed need to germinate. The added shade to the grass crowns insulates them from heat. Finally, a lawn that is left longer will actually grow more slowly. Frequent short shearing triggers growth hormones as the grass races to replace what is lost. Refer to page 61 for recommended mowing heights.

4

GAS-POWERED
LAWN MOWER

MANUAL OR POWERED MOWER?

The most fundamental decision when choosing a lawn mower is whether to buy a manual or powered machine. Mowing is a regular job throughout the spring and summer, so having a mower that is quick and easy to use makes it far less of a chore. The most important factors to consider are:

■ **The size of your lawn** A powered mower is much the better choice for anything but the smallest of lawns, since this type takes out much of the hard work associated with mowing.

■ **Ease of use** A properly sharpened and balanced manual mower is easy to operate, requiring no cables, batteries, or fuel.

■ **Access to power source** Electric lawnmowers require convenient and safe access to an electrical outlet which can be a limiting factor, especially on a large lawn.

■ **Price** Manual mowers are less expensive than powered machines and they do not require gas or electricity to run. However, you will need to have the blades sharpened and balanced annually to ensure that your hand mower continues to function efficiently.

ELECTRICAL SAFETY

• Use a qualified electrician to fit outside electrical sockets.

• Always unplug any electrical equipment before you inspect or clean it.

• Wear strong shoes to protect your feet when using a lawn mower.

• Make sure the outside circuit is protected by a ground-fault circuit interrupter (GFCI).

• When using extension cords for earthed electrical equipment, make sure the extension cord is earthed.

UNDERCARRIAGE OF A LAWN MOWER

4

MANUAL MOWERS

A manual reel or push mower is ideal for a small lawn. The spiral steel blades turn on a reel, catching the grass and cutting it against a fixed blade or bed knife. The resulting cut is very fine.

■ Maintaining a manual mower

A reel mower must be kept properly sharpened and balanced. Have the blades professionally sharpened annually before the spring grass growth spurt. You can adjust the bed knife yourself. Insert a strip of paper between the reel and bed knife, turn the reel by hand, and check that the rotating knife cuts the paper. Raise or lower the bed knife as necessary.

■ Pros and cons

While they are not suitable for a large lawn, manual mowers are perfect for mowing small areas of grass. They purr along quietly, make a fine cut, and take up less storage space than a gas- or electric-powered mower.

POWERED MOWERS

Powered mowers take some of the backache out of lawn mowing. Depending on the model you buy, the power may only turn the blades of the mower, with any forward movement being provided by the person pushing the machine. This type of mower is only one step up from a manual mower.

The majority of powered mowers, however, are self-propelled. The power may be supplied from a number of different sources.

■ Electric

These are usually light, easy to operate, and simple to maintain. They are also relatively quiet and cause no pollution at the point of use. However, they have limited power, so are most suitable for small- to medium-sized lawns.

The major drawback of an electrically powered mower is that it may only be operated within reach of an electric socket. The trailing cable is also inconvenient and potentially hazardous. Accidents may occur if the cable is accidentally cut by the mower blades, exposing live electric wires. Before buying, always check that any outdoor electrical equipment is protected by a ground-fault circuit interrupter, which cuts off the power automatically in the case of an accident. Remember that electric mowers should be stored in a dry shed or at least covered with a waterproof sheet, since the moisture may cause electrical faults.

■ Battery-powered

Cordless mowers have many of the advantages of electric mowers. They are quiet, clean, and easy to use, while overcoming some of their drawbacks. They can be used where there is no electricity supply, and there is no trailing cord to worry about.

However, the weight of the battery makes them heavier than electric mowers, and the battery provides limited power. Most battery-powered mowers run for about one-and-a-half to two hours on one charge, and cut a lawn of approximately 15,000 sq. ft (1,400 sq. m); buying two batteries extends the area that you can cut at one time but inevitably

---

Warning

When using an electric lawn mower, pass the trailing cord over your shoulder to keep it away from the mowing blades. Alternatively, you can buy a special harness to keep the cord out of the way.

adds to the initial outlay. Fully recharging the batteries takes about 20 hours for each battery, but most can be charged sufficiently for use in a much shorter time. The batteries usually last for five years or more before they need replacing.

■ **Gas** Powerful enough for the toughest grass-cutting jobs, gas mowers are very useful if there is no access to an electricity supply. A wide range of models is available.

Gas mowers are heavier and more expensive than electric mowers, however, and require a greater level of maintenance than electric or battery-powered models to keep them running smoothly. Gas mowers also tend to be relatively noisy and produce the same pollutants as a combustion engine.

■ **Solar** Solar-powered mowers appeared on the market relatively recently. Consequently, they are not so readily available and are also significantly more expensive than other powered mowers.

Powered exclusively by a solar panel, "robot" mowers cut grass automatically within a predetermined area. Their most obvious advantage is that they require much less physical effort than either manual or other powered mowers, since they do not need to be pushed. They are also pollution free and therefore more environmentally friendly than gas and electric mowers.

ACHIEVING A BALANCE
A well-tended lawn complements the shrub borders, while its sweeping curves emphasize the tall shapes of the trees.

4

TYPES OF MOWER

L awn mowers cut grass using either cylindrical or rotary blades. Rotary blades are more versatile than cylindrical blades; they can cut wet grass and even tall weeds that a reel mower cannot handle. On the other hand, the cylindrical blades of a reel mower give a finer cut than most rotary blades.

REEL MOWERS

Powered models are the first choice for professional greenkeepers, but the average homeowner is satisfied with a hand-powered version. The rotating blades are fixed in a spiral around a cylinder, and work by cutting against a fixed bottom blade with a scissor action. Push mowers have from five to eight blades; the more blades, the finer the cut. Reel mowers are ideal for high-quality lawns since they give a close, fine cut. However, the blades must be correctly adjusted in order to achieve a good finish. The moving blades should just "kiss" the fixed blade evenly all along its length.

Reel mowers work best on even ground with short- to medium-length grass. You can adjust the height of the cut by raising the blades relative to the front roller. Many reel mowers have a heavy rear roller, which produces the alternating light and dark green stripes that many gardeners like to see on a freshly cut lawn.

ROTARY MOWERS

A rotary mower is supported on wheels and has blades that spin horizontally to cut the grass. The scythelike action is more likely to tear the blades of grass than the clean-cutting scissor action of the reel mower. This type of machine is more suitable than the reel mower models for long grass. It also is better able to cope with bumpy, uneven lawns and slopes. Adjust the height of the cut by setting the height of the blade relative to the wheels.

Depending on the design, a rotary mower may throw the clippings out the side, rear, or front of the machine. A grass collection box or bag is worth the investment for times when the grass is too long to leave the clippings in place. If you do not have a collection box or bag attached to the mower, make sure that the exit chute is not pointed toward a building or any living thing. It is not uncommon for the machines to throw out a rock, which at high speed becomes a dangerous projectile. Rear-throw mowers must have a bag to collect the clippings.

GRASS COLLECTION BOX

4

OTHER TYPES OF MOWER

■ **Mulching mower** This machine is a rotary mower equipped with an extra blade that cuts the grass and leaves into fine particles. The mower blows the clippings back on to the lawn as a mulch, adding valuable organic material. Most models are equipped with a grass catcher to collect clippings when they are too long for effective mulching. Also use a mulching mower to collect fallen leaves off the lawn in the fall; it will chop them roughly to speed up decomposition.

■ **Ride-on mowers** Best suited to large lawns, ride-on mowers have 6–10 horsepower engines and attachments to mow, mulch, and collect grass clippings.

A lawn tractor has an 8–12 horsepower engine and includes up to three rotary blades to cut swaths as wide as 42 in (105 cm). Neither machine is useful in confined areas.

■ **Fly or hover mowers** These are a type of rotary mower, with the same horizontally spinning blade. However, instead of being supported on wheels, the mower hovers slightly above the

HOVER
MOWER

grass on a cushion of air, making it particularly light and easy to maneuver. Hover mowers are good for cutting grass in awkward corners, under overhanging trees and shrubs, and even on uneven lawns and shallow slopes. Although gas-driven hover mowers are available, they are much less popular than electric models.

4

LAWN MOWER MAINTENANCE

Take good care of your lawn mower to ensure many years of efficient service.

• To extend engine wear, change the oil every 25 operating hours. Remember to clean out the air filter too. If you are not comfortable working with engines, have the mower serviced once a year, preferably in winter before the spring rush.

• Drain unused fuel from gas-powered mowers at the end of the mowing season.

• Store the mower in a dry place or shield it from rain with a waterproof covering.

• Have the blade sharpened regularly or replace damaged plastic blades.

ROTARY MOWER BLADES

MOWING

E xcessive mowing frequency reduces total shoot yield, root and rhizome production, and food reserves. With each cut you should aim to remove no more than one-third of the existing green foliage. For example, Kentucky bluegrass should be kept at about 2 in (5 cm) tall; cut back with the mower when it reaches 3 in (8 cm).

MOWING TECHNIQUES

Ideally grass should be dry when you cut it. Wet grass tends to bend over preventing the mower blades from cutting the full height. The resulting open wounds are particularly susceptible to fungal disease in wet conditions. Wet grass also leaves outlines of wheel marks. Remove any debris lying on the lawn as well as ornaments. Steppingstones become easily hidden in long grass so make a note of their whereabouts to avoid damaging the mower on them. Set the blades to the correct height (see opposite) before you start.

■ Every time the grass is cut, wound hormones are produced that promote healing. The grass uses food reserves to fuel the energy required to produce these healing compounds. If you cut the lawn with a blunt blade, the grass will have a ragged cut edge that turns brown, looking unsightly. More important for the sake of the health of your lawn, any torn wounds require more wound healing compounds, obtained from the food reserves stored by the grass. Eventually these reserves are exhausted and the grass is unable to repair the wound, leaving it an open site for fungal entry and serious disease problems.

■ **Change mowing patterns frequently** If you follow the same path and direction every time that you mow, you are likely to get tire ruts in the lawn. Also, grass tends to lean after it is cut; by changing your mowing patterns from time to time, the grass will stand more upright.

4

GRASS CUTTINGS

TIMBER-RING STEPPINGSTONE

HEIGHT OF CUT

Different grass types have different optimum heights. If you have a grass mix that requires several different mowing heights, opt for the height that encourages the most desirable grass. For example, in transitional parts of the United States, Bermuda grass and perennial rye are often mixed, and each has a different ideal height. Cool-season grasses are less aggressive growers, so they need to be cut to their ideal height to have a fighting chance.

The US Lawn Institute recommends the following mowing heights for individual grass species:

■ **Mowing height of 2 in (5 cm)** Recommended for Blue Grama grass; Buffalo grass; Fine fescue; Perennial ryegrass; St. Augustine grass; and Tall fescue.

■ **Mowing height of 1 in (2.5 cm)** Recommended for Bermuda grass; Centipede grass; and Zoysia grass.

GRASS CLIPPINGS AND LEAVES

Generally grass clippings should be left on the lawn where they quickly decompose, adding nutrients to the soil and reducing the need to fertilize by up to two-thirds. Rake up any fallen leaves as soon as possible since they smother the lawn. They are best recycled to make leaf mold. The following are exceptions to leaving the grass clippings where they fall:

Soil lacking microorganisms If the soil is "dead," lacking the microbes and earthworms to break down the grass clippings, then the clippings can build up to cause thatch.

Grass grown too long Occasionally it is necessary to cut off more grass at a time than is ideal. If the grass clippings clump together, collect them up and add them to the garden compost.

Existing thatch problem Collect grass clippings until you have an established thatch problem under control.

COMPOSTED GRASS

LEAF MOLD

4

TOOLS AND EQUIPMENT

Some pieces of equipment are essential for looking after a lawn; others, while not vital, help to make life easier. Choose all items of equipment with care, making sure that they are durable. You should also clean and service them regularly to keep them in good condition.

ESSENTIAL EQUIPMENT

■ **Lawn mower** Buy the best you can afford, making sure you select the type that best suits your specific lawn (see pp. 54–59).

■ **Shears** Long-handled edging shears are easier to use than standard ones for trimming grass edges. Make sure they have a smooth action, and keep the blades sharp.

■ **Half-moon edging iron** You can make do with a sharp, straight-bladed spade, but an edging iron is much easier to use.

■ **Rake** A spring-tined rake is essential to sweep up fallen leaves in the fall. It also helps break up developing thatch.

■ **Watering equipment** A hose and sprinkler is the minimum equipment needed. In dry climates, use a sprinkling system with an automatic timer.

4

TROWEL

HAND FORK

DAISY GRUBBER

NARROW TROWEL

FORK

SPADE

HALF-MOON EDGING IRON

WHEELBARROW

FERTILIZER SPREADER

USEFUL EXTRAS

■ **Nylon-line trimmer** Use this to deal with grass around the feet of trees or the base of walls and fences. They can also be used to edge paths and beds (see pp. 64–65).

■ **Fertilizer spreader** Ensures even distribution and doubles as a seed spreader. Drop and rotary types are available; each has advantages.

■ **Leaf-sweeper/blower** Useful for gathering up fallen debris. Some models blow debris, others double as a vacuum and mulcher as well.

■ **Hose-end sprayers** The easiest method of applying liquid lawn feed or broadleaf weed killer.

■ **Aerator** Special aerating shoes with spikes are quicker to use than manual aerators which require a lot of work. For large jobs, rent an aerator machine that lifts out the cores of soil.

■ **Rotary edger** Hand edging tool with multi-toothed rotary blades that run between a hard edge and the grass to cut a clean, trenched edge.

4

LUXURY ITEMS

Dethatcher If you use proper maintenance techniques, you should not need to dethatch your lawn more than once every two or three years at most. Renting the machine makes the most sense.

Powered edger This is an effortless way to have a professionally edged

lawn. One manufacturer has developed a powered edger that attaches to a rotary tiller motor, saving a little storage space and money.

Garden tractor A tractor is undeniably useful on a large property. Check out extra attachments such as dethatchers and spreaders.

EDGING AND TRIMMING

No matter how beautifully a lawn has been mown, it never looks complete unless the edges have been neatly trimmed. You can do this quite satisfactorily by hand using a pair of long-handled edging shears. On a large lawn you will get the job done much more quickly with a powered edging machine or nylon-line trimmer.

USING EDGING TOOLS

■ **Edging lawns** In spring, the edges of your lawn may need recutting with a sharp edging iron to neaten them. Use a wooden plank laid on the lawn to cut the straight edges against, standing on the plank as you work to keep it in place. Take off the minimum amount of turf necessary for a well-defined finish, otherwise the area of lawn will gradually diminish over time.

Each time you mow, keep the edges neat by using shears or a nylon-line trimmer to cut off overhanging grass

LAWN EDGING
Edging bricks laid flush with the lawn surface facilitate mowing and edging, and help to protect the lawn edges from foot traffic on the path.

afterward. Edges are prone to damage and may need to be repaired (see p. 52).

■ **Awkward corners** Grass may look untidy in places that the mower will not reach, for example around the base of a tree or along the foot of a fence or wall. Use flat shears or a nylon-line trimmer to trim grass here.

Better still, make a grass-free area immediately around the base of trees or large bushes growing on the lawn. To bring all of the grass within reach of the mower, establish a narrow paved mowing strip along the base of walls and fences. Any bare soil may be topped with a layer of gravel or pebbles.

4

TIP
Your lawn will be easier to mow and edge if you keep the shape simple. Complex curves and indentations increase the length of lawn edge considerably. Avoid planting the lawn up against walls and fences. Where suitable, install a hard-surface border along the lawn at ground level so the mower wheel can run along that and the blades will catch every bit of grass. Mulch around trees growing in lawns to avoid nicking the trunk with the mower and to save you having to trim the grass around the trunk.

TIP

Plastic or corrugated metal strips are an inexpensive way to edge a lawn along a bed. They help keep the grass from spreading into the bed and clearly define the boundary between the two areas.

ROLLED
EDGING STRIP

TRIMMING
A string trimmer is a quick and easy way to tidy up lawn edges and to trim in spots where the mower cannot reach.

EDGING

Allowing a lawn to extend all the way to the edge of a path or drive creates difficulties with mowing and edging. As a result, the grass along the lawn edges is likely to become unkempt and straggly, with weeds

taking hold. It is much better to remove a strip of turf and replace it with another material such as gravel, which not only looks attractive but also discourages weeds and does not interfere with mowing.

4

1 First remove any weeds growing in the soil along the lawn edge. Use a trowel, lifting as much of the roots as possible to stop the weeds regrowing.

2 Place a 1–2-in (2.5–5-cm) thick layer of gravel on the soil surface, finishing slightly below the height of the lawn for ease of mowing.

WATERING

All plants, including grass, need a steady supply of water to survive. The amount of water required by your lawn will vary, depending on the degree of drought resistance of the grass species used, the time of year, and the prevailing weather conditions.

WHY WATER YOUR LAWN?

When a lawn does not receive enough water, its growth rate slows down. Eventually, the plant wilts as there is not enough available water to keep the cells of the shoots turgid, or upright; if water is still lacking, the grass then turns brown and falls dormant. It revives when normal watering resumes.

Grass takes up water from the soil through its roots. The water is then transported through a system of veins to all parts of the plant. The water is used by the plant for various vital functions, such as photosynthesis. It also evaporates from exposed surfaces in order to regulate temperature. Water evaporates most readily in hot, dry, windy weather and from large, flat areas (such as leaves). Since grass leaves are very slender, they are quite

well adapted to minimizing water loss through evaporation, but the sheer density of grass shoots present in a lawn can result in a surprising amount of moisture loss from the area as a whole.

Moisture that has been lost through evaporation is replaced naturally by rain and dew. In some conditions, however, there is insufficient moisture from these natural sources to keep the grass from growing. Artificial watering becomes necessary to prevent deterioration of the lawn.

In some climates watering will always be necessary, while in others rainfall may be adequate in most years. The quality and type of soil, as well as the species of grass growing in your lawn, will influence the amount of watering required.

4

SAVING WATER

Water is becoming an increasingly scarce resource. You can reduce the amount of water that your lawn needs to a minimum by:

• Improving the structure of your soil before you plant your lawn

• Choosing drought-resistant grass varieties

• Mowing to the correct height for your grass variety

• Reducing thatch and soil compaction

• Watering infrequently and deeply

• Reducing or eliminating nitrogen fertilizer and increasing potassium fertilizer

• Leaving the clippings on the lawn as you mow. As they decompose, the clippings will release valuable nutrients that will boost the lawn's reserves.

HOW MUCH WATER?

■ **Calculating quantities** Each time you water the lawn, give 1–1½ in (2.5–4 cm) of water to penetrate 6–8 in (15–20 cm) into the soil. In general, 1 in (2.5 cm) of water will penetrate about 12 in (30 cm) in sandy soil, 7 in (18 cm) in loam, and 4–5 in (10–12 cm) in clay. To work out how much water you have given, space containers around the lawn when you sprinkle, and measure the water that collects.

■ **Avoiding waste** If thatch is thicker than ½ in (1 cm), or if the soil is highly compacted, water will run off because it cannot penetrate the soil easily. If you notice run-off, stop the sprinklers and wait for the existing water to soak in. In extreme clay, it can take up to 5 hours for enough water to penetrate. Water for 10 minutes, or until runoff begins, turn off the sprinklers and wait an hour, then water again. Continue until the soil has soaked up at least 1–1½ in (2.5–4 cm) of water.

CENTER OF ATTENTION
A lush, green lawn is enclosed by flowerbeds containing varied collections of herbaceous plants, dwarf conifers, and pots of annuals.

4

WATERING METHODS

During dry seasons, water grass deeply every 7 to 10 days. Color change and reduced resilience are warning signs that grass needs water. If the grass stays flattened when walked on, it is time to water. The best time of day to water is early in the morning; watering in the evening creates the damp conditions that promote disease. Choose a still day to avoid wind evaporation and blowing the water off course.

WATERING RESTRICTIONS

In extreme drought, many communities place watering restrictions until the rains resume. In those cases, it becomes illegal to water your lawn. Do not despair when the grass looks unsightly or turns brown. The grass is dormant, not dead. If the lawn goes dormant, let it stay that way until it naturally greens up again. Too many fluctuations between dormancy and active growth can weaken grass.

WATERING
CAN

HAND-HELD HOSE

Watering with a hose is extremely time consuming and you do not get an even distribution of water. This approach to grass watering makes the most sense if you are keeping a small area of reseeded or returfed grass moist on a daily basis until the new grass is established. Use a nozzle which produces a fine spray of water droplets, playing it over the area as evenly as possible.

4

GARDEN
HOSE

AUTOMATIC TIMERS

An automatic timer is a valuable accessory for a lawn sprinkler system. The timer turns the sprinkler on and off automatically according to a preprogrammed schedule. Timers vary from mechanisms that turn the water on for a set amount of time each day to computerized models that can be programmed to follow a detailed watering schedule.

It is particularly valuable when you are away from home on vacation. When using an automatic timer, a rain meter can help you to assess water intake. This device measures rainfall and turns off the sprinkler when a predetermined amount of rain has been received.

SPRINKLERS

Sprinklers are the most sensible way to water a lawn unless you live in very dry regions of the southwest where homeowners flood their lawns periodically to water deeply with a minimum of evaporation.

■ **In-ground system** An in-ground watering system is almost essential if you live in a dry, hot climate and want to keep your lawn consistently green. Pop-up sprinklers are attached to underground pipes at regular intervals throughout the lawn, spaced to give complete coverage with water spray. Water pressure pushes the sprinkler head above the level of the grass so the spray is not blocked, and the head drops back to ground level when the water stops.

■ **Static** A static sprinkler has a static sprinkler head. Some rest directly on the ground and spray in a circle, others have a spike you push into the lawn. These may spray in quarter, half, or three-quarter circles. They are designed to use in corners.

■ **Impulse (impact)** A strong jet of water is produced from a nozzle head mounted on a sled or spike. The water pressure operates a spring-loaded counterweight, which pushes the sprinkler head round in a series of pulses to cover a circle (or part circle). It is quick, efficient, and covers a large area well.

■ **Rotating (swirl)** This sprinkler has two or three rotating arms on a sled-type base. The arms are driven round by water pressure, and throw water droplets in a wider circle than static sprinklers.

■ **Oscillating** Most convenient for geometrically shaped lawns, this type of sprinkler has an horizontal, perforated sprayline bar that moves backward and forward in a 180° arc.

■ **Traveling** This is a rotating sprinkler with wheels. It is first attached to a garden hose that has been laid out in the required watering pattern. Water pressure from another hose powers both the rotating arms and the wheels. The sprinkler stops moving and watering as soon as it reaches a shut-off ramp.

■ **Pop-up** This is the best system when regular, frequent watering is needed. It should be installed before the lawn is laid, and consists of a grid of underground pipes attached to sprinkler heads that are set just below the lawn surface.

4

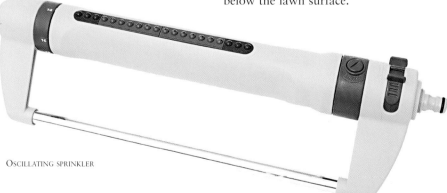

OSCILLATING SPRINKLER

USING FERTILIZERS

If the grass is growing in well-drained soil rich in humus, your lawn will need little extra fertilizer. This is particularly true if you leave the grass clippings on the lawn when you mow. The clippings provide organic matter to the soil and encourage earthworms which produce fertile castings and aerate the soil as they burrow.

WHY FEED YOUR LAWN?

All living plants need a supply of nutrients from the soil to be able to survive and flourish. Their needs include the major nutrients, that is, nitrogen, phosphorus, and potassium, as well as minor nutrients such as iron, manganese, and copper. A rich, humus soil should contain all these nutrients. However, repeated mowing will drain the food reserves stored by the grass. Also, not all lawns are raised in ideal conditions and so rely on regular applications of soil amendments. It is a good idea to plan on fertilizing your lawn at least once a year.

HEAVY-DUTY GARDENING GLOVES

Be aware, however, that overfeeding can be as damaging to a lawn as underfeeding. A sudden boost of nitrogen (a common way of feeding lawns in spring) encourages lush leaf growth at the expense of roots. This creates thatch, weakening the overall plant, and encouraging weeds. Instead, you should aim to encourage a strong root system that will in turn support healthy top growth. The best way to achieve this goal is with a slow-release nitrogen in a balanced fertilizer blend.

It is worthwhile having the soil in your lawn tested every three years by a professional laboratory. As well as assessing your soil pH, the resulting report will tell you exactly what nutrients are missing and recommend how much and what kind of fertilizer you need to resolve the problem.

LIGHTWEIGHT GARDENING GLOVES

FEEDS AND FEEDING TIMES

The ideal lawn food is an organic material such as composted manure. In addition to providing a complex blend of nutrients that have more long-term benefits than quick-acting concentrated fertilizers, you are building the soil. Commercial organic fertilizers are more expensive than the synthetic blends, but in the long run your lawn will perform better.

Chemical fertilizers often contain larger amounts of nutrients than organic fertilizers and are cheaper to buy. However, the fast-released nitrogen is more apt to burn foliage and leach out of the soil. In addition, the salts in synthetic fertilizers will kill off beneficial organisms in the soil, including earthworms.

When to apply fertilizer depends on the type of grass.

■ **Cool-season grasses** Fall is the most important time to fertilize. It is a time of year when grass is growing vigorously, as well as storing nutrients for next spring. If the grass is ailing and your soil is poor, give a light feeding in spring as well.

■ **Warm-season grasses** When growth picks up in spring, fertilize these lawns. Bermuda and Zoysia also respond well to an extra feeding in early fall, but do not feed any warm-season grass later in the fall as you will interrupt the natural slowing for winter dormancy.

LIQUID FERTILIZER

GRANULAR FERTILIZER

4

MAJOR PLANT NUTRIENTS

Nitrogen (N) Promotes thick, vigorous growth and a deep green color. Too much nitrogen encourages excessive growth and increases the need to mow. It produces thin-walled blade cells prone to injury and disease.

Phosphorus (P) Encourages healthy, vigorous roots and good shoot

production. It tends to remain in the soil, so it is often not necessary to add more to the lawn.

Potassium (K) Produces strong roots, hardiness, disease resistance, and good hard-wearing qualities in turf. More prone than phosphorus to leach from the soil.

APPLYING FERTILIZERS

There are several different ways to distribute fertilizers. Quick-release, high-nitrogen chemical fertilizers can burn plants, whereas water-insoluble nitrogen fertilizers release the nitrogen into the soil slowly over a period of time.

APPLICATION METHODS

Choose the method of applying fertilizer that best meets your needs based on the size of your lawn, the type of fertilizer you prefer using, and the amount of storage space you have for garden equipment. Water in dry fertilizers if rain does not fall within 48 hours after spreading.

■ **Hand broadcasting** You can toss dry, pelleted fertilizer around your lawn by hand. Use the same technique you would for scattering seed by hand (see p. 28–31). Measure out the correct dose of fertilizer and divide it between suitably sized areas of lawn for an even distribution.

WHEELED FERTILIZER SPREADER

■ **Drop spreaders** One of the easiest ways to apply dry fertilizer to a lawn, drop spreaders allow the fertilizer to trickle through calibrated holes at the base of the hopper. Read the fertilizer package instructions to find out which calibration gives the appropriate distribution for your brand of spreader.

When using a drop spreader, overlap the wheels on each pass to avoid missing a narrow strip. At the same time, be careful not to overlap too much, as you risk burning the grass. To avoid dropping fertilizer accidentally, close the spreader when you are turning around at the end of a row, when you are stopped, and when you are moving backward. If a spill occurs, sweep up as much of the fertilizer as you can, and then water in the rest thoroughly.

■ **Broadcast spreaders** As the name suggests, a broadcast spreader casts out the material from a rotating disk at the bottom of the hopper. You will

Warning

A uneven application of high-nitrogen lawn fertilizer will result in a streaky lawn with missed areas looking less lush and a taking on a paler green color. Too heavy an application of quick-release nitrogen can scorch or even kill the grass.

4

distribute more fertilizer with each pass of a broadcast spreader than a drop spreader, making the job quicker. If, however, you are using a fertilizer that includes broadleaf herbicides, you don't want the poisons to get into nearby flowerbeds. The herbicide doesn't know the difference between a weed and a desirable ornamental. Know how wide the spreader throws out the material so you can space your passes appropriately.

■ **Hose-end sprayers** Apply liquid fertilizers with a sprayer attached to the hose. Carefully read the instructions for both the sprayer jar and the fertilizer so you get the correct proportion of fertilizer to water. Be sure the sprayer is working correctly with no clogged spray holes.

Slow- and fast-release

Nitrogen fertilizers come in two types: water-soluble or water-insoluble. Water-soluble nitrogen, such as uncoated urea, ammonium nitrate, calcium nitrate, ammonium phosphate, and ammonium sulfate, are released into the soil as soon as they are watered. Results are almost instantaneous, turning the grass a vivid green. However you risk burning the grass, and if you get a heavy rain or water frequently, the nitrogen will continue to move through the soil until it has leached away completely.

In contrast, slow-release nitrogen fertilizers, including sulfur-coated

urea, methylene urea, activated sludge, dried poultry waste, and isobutylidene diurea (IBDU), release the nitrogen over time, gently dosing the lawn throughout the growing season. Slow-release fertilizers tend to be more expensive, but they do not leach away.

To keep your lawn healthy, fertilize cool-season grasses at an annual rate of about 2 lb (1 kg) of nitrogen per 1,000 sq. ft (90 sq. m). Apply two-thirds in the fall and one-third in spring. Warm-season grasses benefit from 2–4 lb (1–2 kg) of nitrogen per 1,000 sq. ft (90 sq. m) annually. Your lawn's feeding needs are influenced by soil quality and texture and by whether or not you leave your grass clippings on the lawn.

APPLYING LIQUID FERTILIZER
You can buy attachments for use with liquid fertilizers that are fitted to the end of a garden hose, making application much more efficient.

4

LAWN SAND

Warning

Take care when applying lawn sand; too high a concentration will damage the grass. In addition, you should avoid walking on treated lawns for a day or two, until the powder has been washed in, since excess foot traffic will leave black footprints.

SOIL AERATION

It is vital to have oxygen in the soil for the healthy development of the grass's roots and the proper functioning of essential soil micro-organisms. The amount of oxygen present depends on a number of factors, the most important being soil type and degree of compaction.

SOIL TYPES

■ **Sandy soil** Light, sandy soil is unlikely to need aerating. It consists of large particles that have relatively large spaces between them, allowing water to drain away quickly.

■ **Clay soil** Heavy clay soil consists of tiny particles with only small spaces between them; water is easily retained around the soil particles, filling all the spaces and reducing the amount of air in the soil. Lawns growing on clay soil are likely to need aerating to improve growth.

■ **Compacted soil** Soil compaction is caused by frequent foot or other traffic, and heavy soils are more likely to be badly affected.

UNDERSTATED FORMALITY
The large expanse of lawn is clearly the main focus of this formal garden, with two stately trees providing welcome shade.

4

AERATION METHODS

Spiking, slitting, and hollow tining all help to relieve compaction and introduce air to the roots of a lawn. These techniques also allow soil conditioners and water to penetrate the lawn surface more easily. All these operations should be carried out only when necessary, rather than on a routine basis.

■ **Hollow tining** This is the best method to use on heavy, highly compacted soil. In early fall, when the soil is moist, remove a series of solid plugs of turf and the soil beneath them. The holes should be approximately ½ in (1 cm) across and up to 4 in (10 cm) deep, spaced about 4 in (10 cm) apart. The job can be done with a hollow tine fork, which you push into the turf with your foot. Coring machines with hollow tines on a revolving drum make the job easier over a large area. Sweep up the cores and add them to the compost heap. After a few days top-dress the lawn with a mixture of sand and compost.

You may only need to carry out hollow tining on small areas of the lawn, and even this is rarely necessary every year.

■ **Spiking** This method, which is also best carried out in the fall, creates holes in the lawn but does not remove any soil plugs. It is useful on moderately compacted areas.

On small lawns you can use a garden fork, inserting the tines straight into the soil to a depth of approximately 4 in (10 cm), rocking the fork forward and backward to open up the holes. On larger areas, it is better to use a hand-operated or powered spiking machine – the length of the spikes may vary from ½–4 in (1–10 cm).

SPIKING THE LAWN
Making a series of small holes in the turf allows air to reach the roots of the grass and also relieves soil compaction.

4

■ **Slitting** A slitting machine consists of sharp, V-shaped blades fitted to rows of wheels and is pushed across the turf. The blades slice through to a depth of about 3 in (8 cm). The machines may be manual or powered. They are quicker and easier to use than either spiking or coring machines because of the slicing action of the blades but do not produce such good aeration.

Slitting is the best method for relieving surface compaction and does not disturb the turf as much as hollow tining or spiking. Use a slitting machine in moist conditions on compacted areas from mid-summer to late fall, as necessary.

DETHATCHING

Thatch is undecomposed organic matter that builds up on the lawn at soil level. Stoloniferous grasses such as Zoysia grass are very prone to thatch, but any lawn can develop the problem if not cared for properly. A small amount of thatch protects the grass from drought and wear, but a thick layer stops air and water reaching the roots, inhibits new shoot production, and increases the risk of disease.

THE DETHATCHING PROCESS

If the soil is alive with beneficial microorganisms, dead plant material at the base of the grass shoots will decompose on its own. A thatch problem begins when quick-release nitrogen fertilizers promote too much top growth that cannot decompose fast enough, while at the same time killing off the earthworms and microorganisms that stimulate decomposition. Compacted soil and shallow, frequent watering encourage grass roots to stay near the soil surface, also contributing to thatch. With patience, you can reduce thatch without ruining your lawn. Generally, however, it takes two to three years, depending on how thick the thatch layer is.

Your primary goal is to encourage microbe activity. Plan to aerate your lawn twice a year, in fall and spring. Before you aerate, spread a top-dressing of compost over the lawn. This will introduce the wanted microbes and enzymes that break down the dead plant material. Water the compost to work it into the soil and near the grass roots. Leave the aerated cores in place. They will quickly break down into the soil. While you are dealing with thatch, collect all grass clippings and use them as mulch or put them in the compost pile. On a small lawn, use a rake to collect the clippings, as the action of raking will help to remove the top layer of thatch.

4

MOWING UP
DEAD GRASS
After scarifying, set the blades of the lawn mower high and mow with the grass box attached to pick up the dead grass and other debris.

DETHATCHING TOOLS

■ **Vertical mower** This machine has a set of vertical blades mounted on a cylinder that spins around. The blades slice through the thatch, thinning it and bringing the cut pieces up to the surface. Watch to make sure the grass is not being ripped out of the soil. This may happen if the grass roots are too shallow. Stop immediately and raise the height of the blades. Set higher, the blades will not cut through as much thatch, but at least the first layer will be removed. If you make a second pass at the lawn with a vertical mower, work at right angles from the direction you first took.

■ **Thatching rake** This is a hand tool especially designed to remove thatch. About 15 in (35 cm) wide, it has 20 curved "teeth" that pull and cut through the matted grass. Models vary.

Some have adjusting heads so you can set the angle to be most comfortable for your height. On another, the cutting edges lock in place as you pull, biting into the thatch to break it up. When you push the rake, the teeth roll under the head so the loosened thatch is released.

■ **Power rake** Useful on a thin layer of thatch, a power rake has steel tines that spin around on a cylinder, grabbing and tearing at the thatch. It is not strong enough to cut through a thick thatch mat.

FANNED LAWN RAKE AT
NARROW SETTING

FANNED LAWN RAKE AT
FULL-WIDTH SETTING

4

WEEDS AND DISEASES

Too many weeds spoil the appearance of a lawn, if they are not controlled. Fortunately, lawn diseases are not so common, but they can still be troublesome if they take hold. Some of the best-known weeds and diseases are dealt with in Chapter 5, but there are several prevention and control techniques that should form part of your annual maintenance program.

PREVENTING WEEDS

The first step in preventing lawn weeds should take place before the lawn is made, by removing all traces of perennial weeds during initial soil cultivation. If you are creating a lawn from seed, you should also allow the first flush of annual weed seeds to germinate, removing them before sowing the seed (see p. 26).

Inevitably, weeds will still appear in an established lawn. Dormant weed seeds remain viable in the soil for many years, and fresh weed seeds are blown in on the wind or dropped by birds and animals. Segments of weeds may also be transferred to a lawn on your shoes or by gardening equipment. Good maintenance

RAKING BEFORE MOWING
It is a good idea to go over the lawn with a rake before mowing, since this helps to ensure that weeds are cut down by the mower blades.

4

WEED INFESTATION
If lawn weeds are not
dealt with promptly,
they will soon spread
to form highly visible
clumps. Your best
option at this stage is
to remove them by
hand, reseeding any
bare patches.

techniques help prevent too many of them from gaining a foothold. Below are some of the key tasks:

■ **Regular mowing** Many broad-leaved weeds are unable to withstand having their topgrowth regularly removed by a lawn mower. They may regenerate once or twice, but regular mowing will eventually kill them.

■ **Mowing correctly** Mowing the lawn too closely weakens the grass, enabling weed species to compete more effectively. Close mowing also increases light penetration to the soil surface, which may encourage the germination of weed seeds.

■ **Change your soil conditions** Avoid weeds by removing the conditions in which they flourish. Bindweed, quick grass, and plantain enjoy compacted soil. Aerate the lawn to discourage them. Ox-eye daisies, foxtail, yellow dock, and horsetails thrive in moist conditions, so improve the drainage to deter them.

■ **Raking before mowing** Some weed species have a flat, rosette-forming, or creeping habit of growth so are not cut down by a lawn mower. Raking the lawn before mowing raises their leaves and stems to meet the blades.

■ **Feeding and watering** Grass that is undernourished or badly affected by drought becomes thin and patchy. Weeds are usually better adapted to adverse conditions than cultivated plants, which is precisely why they become weeds in the first place.

■ **Aerating** Aerating gets oxygen into the soil and reduces its compaction. Both benefits make a more vigorous grass that can compete with weeds.

4

MOSS

The presence of moss often indicates that there is something wrong with the general growing conditions of a lawn. Moss may colonize a shady or damp patch of lawn or an area of low fertility, for example.

Correcting these specific faults is the most effective way of controlling moss, and will at the same time improve the general health and vigor of the grass.

APPLYING WEED KILLERS

Because weeds are such a common problem on lawns, many gardeners apply a herbicide annually on a routine basis. This has been made possible by the development of so-called selective weed killers, which kill many lawn weeds whilst at the same time allowing the grass to remain unharmed. They can therefore be applied over the entire lawn area, not just to the weeds.

It is important to remember that selective weed killers cannot really distinguish between grass and weeds. The narrow leaves of the grass shoots simply do not absorb enough of the chemical weed killer for it to have any appreciative effect. If lawn weed killers are applied at too high a concentration, they will kill the grass as well as the weeds.

■ **When to apply** For the best effect, apply selective weed killers during a period of strong growth; late spring and early summer are the most suitable times. Herbicides are often combined with fertilizer in a "weed-and-feed" mixture. This saves work by doing two jobs at the same time, and also increases the effectiveness of the weed killer. Herbicide may be applied in early

---

Warning

• Selective weed killers are extremely potent and will kill or cause severe distortion in all garden plants other than grasses.

• Take great care when applying them, since they may be carried for long distances on the breeze.

• Make sure that sprayers, watering cans, and spreaders used for applying weed killers are clearly labelled and are not used for any other jobs.

• Weed killer concentrates should not be stored in a greenhouse or near broad-leaved plants, since even the fumes may cause damage.

• Clippings from lawns that have recently been treated with a selective weed killer should not be used as a mulch or for making compost.

---

fall as well as spring, when it should be applied to the lawn on its own, without any fertilizer.

■ **How to apply** Herbicides are available either as liquids, which are diluted and applied with a sprayer, or as powders or granules, which are best applied with a drop spreader (see pp. 72–73). Make sure that the spreader is correctly calibrated for the product you are using, since overdosing can seriously damage the lawn.

APPLYING WEED KILLER TO AN INDIVIDUAL LEAF

DISEASE PREVENTION

Most lawn diseases are caused by fungi and may be controlled with applications of fungicide (see pp. 90–91). However, it is better to prevent the onset of lawn diseases with sound cultural practises.

■ **Use resistant varieties** Grass species and varieties vary in their susceptibility to fungal infections. Choose varieties that are known to have good resistance to most of the common diseases.

■ **Fertilize correctly** Feed grass adequately to promote strong growth, but take care not to overuse nitrogen fertilizers, especially in late summer and fall. Nitrogen promotes soft, lush growth that is particularly prone to disease.

■ **Use good mowing techniques** Mowing increases the lawn's susceptibility to disease because it damages the leaf blades. Minimize the damage by keeping the mower blades sharp. Mowing to the correct height is also important. Grass that is too short will be weakened and less able to resist disease, while long grass creates a humid microclimate that favors disease.

■ **Improve growing conditions** Many fungus diseases are encouraged by damp, humid conditions. Reducing shade and improving drainage by spiking the lawn to aerate it (see p. 75) may help to control the incidence of disease.

■ **Deal with thatch** A build-up of thatch encourages a favorable microclimate for fungal growth. If you have a thatch problem, collect the grass clippings and scarify the lawn to remove the thatch (see pp. 76–77).

FEEDING A LAWN
Carefully weigh out the amount of fertilizer for the area you need to treat, wearing gloves to protect your skin from the harsh chemicals.

4

ANNUAL MAINTENANCE PROGRAM

WARM-SEASON GRASSES: SOUTH

WINTER
• Mow and edge overseeded cool-season grass.

• Service lawn mower, sharpen blades.

SPRING
• Plant new lawn from seeds, plugs, sprigs, or sod; patch worn spots.

• Fertilize when warm-season grasses begin to grow.

• Dethatch the lawn, if necessary.

• Mow overseeded cool-season grass very short to give warm-season grasses a head start.

• Mow and edge; mow often enough that you only remove one-third of the grass blade each time.

• Take necessary measures to control weeds and disease.

SUMMER
• Use broadleaf weed control when weeds are actively growing, but before temperatures get too high.

• Water as needed.

• Mow and edge.

• Feed with liquid fish or seaweed for greening boost.

FALL
• Mow warm-season grass short, fertilize, then overseed with winter rye.

• Aerate.

COOL-SEASON GRASSES: NORTH

WINTER
• Service lawn mower, sharpen blades.

SPRING
• Give a light feeding, about one-third of the annual fertilizer application.

• Plant new lawn from seeds, plugs, springs, or sod; patch worn spots.

• Begin mowing and edging; mow often enough that you only remove one-third of the grass blade each time.

• Dethatch the lawn, if necessary.

• Spread crabgrass control.

• Apply lime to control moss, sorrel, and wild strawberries.

SUMMER
• Use broadleaf weed control when weeds are actively growing, but before temperatures get too high.

• Mow and edge.

• Water as needed.

• Feed with liquid fish or seaweed for greening boost.

FALL
• Aerate.

• Keep leaves raked.

• Spot seed.

• Fertilize (give two-thirds of annual feeding).

• Mow and edge as needed.

4

Controlling lawn problems

What is a weed? 84
Defines weeds in grass and looks at methods of weed control

Lawn weeds 86
Describes the most common lawn weeds, and how to control them, and explains the action of different types of weed killer

Pests and diseases 90
Looks at the most common lawn pests and how to control them, and how to recognize and deal with the most common turf grass diseases

Mowing problems 98
Outlines why poor mowing techniques can cause problems, and offers advice on how to remedy them

Weather damage 100
Explains how excessive rain, drought, frost, snow, and wind can damage a lawn, and how to deal with problems

Shade 102
Looks at the specific problems caused to lawns by shade, and lists cultivars that have been developed to cope with shade

5

CONTROLLING LAWN PROBLEMS

Things sometimes go wrong with even the best maintained lawns. The most commonly encountered problems are caused by weeds. Dandelions are immediately obvious when they spring up on a neat area of grass, but other weeds are more difficult to spot until they have spread widely.

Pests and diseases are not so common on turf, but they can be a major nuisance if they are not controlled. Adverse weather conditions, such as heavy rain or drought, may also create unexpected difficulties. In most cases, by taking prompt action you can prevent the situation from deteriorating farther. Identifying the cause of a problem is the first step toward putting it right.

Sometimes a better understanding of the needs of the grass can prevent problems occurring in the first place. You will avoid having to take remedial action to deal with bare patches and moss proliferation by addressing their causes early on. These include a lack of sunlight and poor air circulation, which is commonly associated with heavy shade.

5

WHAT IS A WEED?

The usual definition of a weed is a plant in the wrong place – and in a lawn, that means any plant other than grass. The definition can even include grass species that are not of the desired lawn type. Weeds are undesirable in lawns because the difference in leaf pattern and color spoils the regular, velvety look and texture of the grass. They also compete with the grass for nutrients and water, weakening the turf.

WEED CONTROL

Lawn weeds are often referred to as broad-leaved weeds. Some, such as plantain and daisy, do indeed have broad leaves, while others, such as yarrow and woodrush, have quite slender or ferny leaves. Non-grass weeds would be a more accurate description for these plants. The distinction in leaf size is made because of the action of selective weed killers. These work on the principle that weeds, having a greater leaf surface, will take up more of the active ingredient than the grass shoots, which survive the treatment without apparent harm.

The majority of non-grass weeds cannot withstand regular mowing. A newly sown lawn may have a high proportion of weed species that germinate at the same time as the grass, but most of them will weaken and die out after the first few cuts. However, weeds with a creeping, low-growing, or rosette-forming growth habit, such as clover, are able to escape the lawn mower's blades. These are the ones that become most troublesome. Some species may not be particularly noticeable during spring and summer while they are green, but in winter they turn yellow or die, resulting in a very patchy appearance on a lawn.

Cultural methods of preventing weed infestation are discussed on pages 78–80, but some weeds may still manage to take hold despite all your best efforts. If the offending weeds are fairly isolated, they may be dealt with individually by spot treatment (see p.80). However, if

5

LAWN CLOVER

TIP

Apply weed killer two to three weeks after feeding the lawn, when the grass and weeds are both growing strongly. You will also get better results if you avoid mowing the lawn for up to three days before and after treatment.

they are allowed to spread across a wide area, an overall lawn treatment will be necessary.

■ **Manual removal** Remove isolated weeds by hand, pulling them from the soil or cutting them out with a trowel. This can be time consuming but it is a good method for annual weeds, as long as you remove them before they produce seeds. It is not such a good method for perennial weeds, however, which regenerate from small portions of root or stem that are inadvertently left behind. Continually removing the topgrowth, however, will eventually weaken the roots even of perennial weeds.

■ **Spot treatment** This method involves treating individual weeds with a herbicide, which you can buy in the form of a ready-to-use spray, wax, or impregnated sponge stick. These contain stronger herbicides than selective weed killers and are therefore more effective against persistent weeds, but they must only be used to treat isolated weeds rather than the whole of the lawn. For organic gardens, there are non-chemical methods for treating isolated weeds. It can be very effective to slash the crowns of weeds or to scorch them with a flame gun.

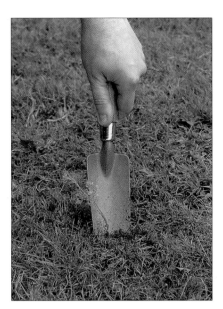

WEEDING WITH A TROWEL
Remove large or rosette-forming weeds with a hand trowel, taking care to lift the root ball as well as the topgrowth.

■ **Overall treatment** This relies on the use of a selective weed killer, that is, one that kills weed species but does not harm the grass (see p. 80). Take care to apply it at the right concentration, otherwise the results will be poor. On badly infested lawns repeat the treatment two or three times during the summer, at four-to-six-week intervals.

5

USING A DAISY GRUBBER
A daisy grubber is a special tool with a sharp, straight prong, which allows you to lever weeds out of your lawn without damaging the turf.

LAWN WEEDS

The following pages describe the most commonly encountered weed species, with suggestions on how to control each type. Some weeds are resistant to one or more herbicides, so nearly all brands of selective weed killer contain two or more active ingredients to broaden their usefulness. To get the best results from a weed killer, identify the type of weeds in your lawn first, then choose your brand accordingly.

TYPES OF WEED KILLER

■ **Selective weed killers** Many brands of selective weed killer (also known as hormone weed killer) are available from hardware stores and garden centers, but they contain only a relatively small number of active ingredients. The range of ingredients includes 2,4–D, dichlorophen, MCPP, dicamba, and mecoprop.

■ **Non-selective weed killers** A herbicide that will kill any vegetation it touches, including your lawn. Use carefully for a spot treatment of narrowleaf weeds when nothing else will work (see p. 85).

■ **Pre-emergent weed killers** Creates a film on the soil surface that stops seed germination. Effective for grassy annual weeds.

WEED-INFESTED LAWN
Several weed species, including chickweed and clover, have taken hold and threaten to overrun this lawn.

Warning

A weed in your lawn indicates that all is not right with the soil or your cultivation practices. Identify the weed, learn the conditions it likes (see pp. 87–89), and then amend the soil and modify your growing practices to deter the weed. For example, cinquefoil indicates acid infertile, sandy soil.

5

COMMON LAWN WEEDS

CHICKWEED
(Cerastium)
The particular species of chickweed that is most often a problem in lawns is called mouse-ear chickweed (C. holosteoides). It is a perennial weed with slender, hairy stems that form a spreading clump, topped with small white flowers. It is most common on dry, limy soils.
CONTROL Selective weed killer mixtures.

CLOVER
(Trifolium species)
Two clover species are common on lawns. White clover (Trifolium repens) has typical trifoliate leaves, with each leaflet marked with a white arc near the base. The rounded flower heads are white, tinged with pink, and are popular with bees. Plants are prostrate, and spread by creeping, rooting runners. Yellow suckling clover, or lesser trefoil (T. dubium), has small, round, yellow flowers. It produces prostrate stems that cover a large area but do not root.
CONTROL Both species can be controlled by selective weed killers, but tend to be resistant to MCPP and 2,4-D.

Yellow suckling clover is the more difficult of the two to eradicate, and needs several treatments. Use a grass box when mowing to prevent the weed from setting seed.

DANDELION
(Taraxacum officinale)
Pointed, jagged leaves form a dense rosette that has a long, thick taproot. Shaggy yellow flowers appear in late spring, followed by seed puffs that scatter to the winds. Cat's ear (Hypochaeris radicata) is often confused with dandelion, but the leaves are hairy and lobed, rather than toothed, and flowers are produced on tall, branching, non-fleshy stems. Control of cat's ear is the same as for dandelion.
CONTROL Dandelions thrive when the grass is thin and cut short. The long taproot will regenerate if bits are left in the soil, but if you persist, eventually they will weaken and die. Young plants are easier to pull than established ones. Pick flowers before they go to seed. Spot-spray with non-selective, systemic herbicide, or use a systemic,

broadleaf herbicide that kills the root as well as the foliage.

ENGLISH DAISY
(Bellis perennis)
The English daisy has tight rosettes of mid-green, spoon-shaped leaves and white-petaled, yellow-centered flowers. A sprinkling of daisy flowers in a home lawn is a pretty sight, but the plants spread rapidly, and can quickly get out of hand. Tolerates low soil fertility.
CONTROL One or two treatments of a selective weed killer mixture containing 2,4-D and dicamba or 2,4-D and MCPP.

GROUND IVY
(Glechoma hederacea)
A perennial, broadleaf creeping weed with rounded, scalloped leaves, a minty smell, and purple flowers. Colonizes in moist, damp shade, but takes sun as well.
CONTROL Improve the soil and lessen the surface moisture. Hand pull plants when they first appear, or rake plants upright in spring and mow close. It may be necessary to resort to using broadleaf herbicide.

5

COMMON LAWN WEEDS

PLANTAIN
(Plantago species)
Several species of plantain are a nuisance in lawns. Great or broad-leaved plantain *(P. major)* has broad, oval, deeply veined leaves that form a large rosette. Slender, pale green, poker-type flowers are borne in summer and will often spring back up after the lawn mower has passed over them. Hoary plantain *(P. media)* has similar leaves with very short leaf stalks and oval-shaped flower heads with prominent stamens. Ribwort *(P. lanceolata)* has narrower leaves than the other two species. Plaintain seeds heavily and will quickly spread if left unchecked.
CONTROL All plantain species can be killed with selective weed killer mixtures containing 2,4-D plus MCPP and dicamba. Spot treatment also is possible. Hand pull when the soil is moist

PURSLANE
(Portulaca oleracea)
An annual mat-forming plant with fleshy, red oblong leaves and stems. Bears small

yellow flowers that ripen into urn-shaped seed capsules that sow prolifically. Likes hot, dry weather and will invade a thin, weak, or new lawn.
CONTROL If your lawn is poison-free, you can harvest the leaves for salads or cooked greens. Get the grass growing vigorously to choke it out. If it gets out of hand, use a broadleaf, post-emergent herbicide.

SPOTTED SPURGE
(Euphorbia maculata)
An annual broadleaf that quickly grows to form a circular mat in the lawn, it tolerates

both fertile and infertile soil, filling in bare patches in the grass. It germinates in late spring and early summer.
CONTROL Either pre-emergent chemical with DCPA or post-emergent weed killer containing 2,4-D and MCPP plus dicamba are effective. It is also easy to hand pull, especially if the soil is moist.

WEED GRASSES
A weed is any grass that does not blend in well with the grass in your lawn because of its texture, color, or growth habit.

CLOVER

5

COMMON LAWN WEEDS

Annual bluegrass
(Poa annua) This shallow-rooted plant sprouts in early spring and sets seed in late spring, then resprouts and goes to seed again in the fall. It likes cool, moist conditions and will grow in infertile, compacted soil. In summer, it wilts, opening up space for other weeds.
CONTROL Improve soil, hand pull, use pre-emergent herbicide.

Crabgrass *(Digitaria species)* A sun-loving annual that thrives on a thin, overwatered lawn in the heat of midsummer. Fertilizing cool-season lawns in midsummer actually feeds the actively growing crabgrass while the dormant cool-season grass receives nothing.
CONTROL Make sure that your lawn is growing densely in early spring before the crabgrass seeds germinate. Mow high; the shade of thick, tall grass will stop most of the crabgrass seeds from sprouting or growing. For heavy infestations, use a safe-for-grass-seed pre-emergent chemical in mid-spring. Remove seed heads to prevent further spread.

OXALIS
(*Oxalis stricta/ O. europaea*)
Perennial, broadleaf weeds with pale green cloverlike foliage and small five-petaled yellow flowers. Will grow in sun or shade. Spreads with creeping, rooting stems and prolific seed production.
CONTROL Oxalis grows in compacted soils, so you can discourage it by improving soil conditions. Try pre-emergent control with oxadiazon or siduron, selective weed killer 2,4-D plus MCPP and dicamba, or spot treat with nonselective glyphosate.

YARROW
(*Achillea millefolium*)
The presence of yarrow in your lawn indicates poor soil fertility. The ferny, aromatic leaves form a pale green rosette. Creeping underground stems ensure that the plant spreads rapidly. Clusters of white or pink-tinged flowers appear in summer.
CONTROL A difficult weed to control, since yarrow is resistant to MCPP and 2,4-D. Repeated applications of selective weed killer mixtures are necessary for successful results. Rake the lawn before mowing to lift the weeds to meet the blades. Improve fertility by feeding and top-dressing regularly. Water the grass during dry weather.

THISTLE GRASS

5

PESTS AND DISEASES

Grass does not suffer from attack by pests and diseases to the same degree as other plants, but they may still cause a lot of damage and are difficult to treat effectively. The following pages describe the most common pests and diseases, with suggestions on their control.

CONTROLLING PESTS

Lawns pose a special problem for insecticide application. The size of most lawns means that relatively large quantities of chemicals need to be used, and the insecticide is rapidly washed through the turf and soil, leading to contamination of water supplies. For this reason, you should only use them as a last resort when other methods have failed to control the problem.

In some cases, cultural techniques may be used to reduce or eliminate a pest problem. Occasionally, biological controls are successful. In other cases, there is little that can be done to control the pest. Fortunately, most gardeners are unlikely ever to experience a serious pest problem.

TURF GRASS DISEASES

Fungi are the most common cause of turf diseases. Pathogenic (disease-causing) fungi are often parasitic, living off the nutrients manufactured by plants. Such parasitism weakens the turf but is not usually the source of greatest damage; fungi also produce harmful substances such as toxins and enzymes, which interfere with the essential metabolic processes carried out by the plants.

■ **Pathogenic fungi** These usually arrive on a new plant in the form of spores, which soon germinate and enter the tissues of the plant, often through wounds. The disease continues to develop within the

Warning

Many of the insecticides that were once standard remedies for treating a range of lawn pests are now no longer available to amateur gardeners. Such insecticides have had to be withdrawn in several countries because of their persistence in the soil and the potential damage they could cause to wildlife, such as birds and insects, and the natural environment.

infected plant, and eventually produces more spores that go on to attack new plants.

Mowing unavoidably produces a large quantity of wounded tissue on the grass shoots, making the turf particularly susceptible to infection by pathogens. Given that this is so, it is surprising that diseases are not more prevalent on lawns. However, environmental conditions need to be just right for a pathogen before it can start to develop; most pathogens thrive in conditions of high humidity.

■ **Minimizing the damage** You can cut down the likelihood of a disease taking hold of your lawn by improving the growing conditions and always using good cultural techniques (see opposite). Early detection and treatment are the best methods of dealing with lawn diseases, to prevent the infection spreading any farther. Generally, the most effective method is to treat the area with a systemic fungicide such

5

as carbendazim. However, not all diseases affecting lawns respond well to the use of fungicides. To avoid the unnecessary use of chemicals you need to be sure you have made the correct diagnosis. Before you begin, seek professional advice if you are in any doubt.

IDENTIFYING PROBLEM AREAS
Shaded and poorly drained lawns, especially in sheltered positions with little air circulation, are the most vulnerable to pests and diseases.

CULTURAL CONTROLS

Establishing a good lawn maintenance program of regular mowing, watering, and feeding will significantly reduce the risk of infection from diseases (see Chapter 4). Improving growing conditions by, for example, reducing shade (see p.102) and installing drainage ditches (p. 25) on waterlogged sites, will also help.

5

COMMON LAWN PESTS

Leatherjackets Most commonly occurring in wet weather and on badly drained soils, leatherjackets are the larvae of crane flies, or daddy-long-legs. Adult females lay their eggs in the lawn in summer. The gray, legless larvae hatch out in summer and fall, feeding on grass roots throughout fall, winter, and spring. Heavy infestations can create large patches of severely weakened grass, which turns yellow or brown under stress and may die.

White grubs These are the larvae of a number of beetles and chafers. Normally they are cream colored with a brown head and a dark area on their posterior. They are usually curled up in a distinctive "C" shape. They eat grass roots, causing brown areas in the lawn. When that happens, you can roll back the turf like a rug to reveal the grubs.
CONTROL Treat the lawn with milky spore or parasitic nematodes.

Chinch bugs Common in both the north and south, adults have a black triangle between their folded white wings. The nymphs have a black head followed by a white stripe and a red tail. They love thatch, nesting there and then venturing out to suck the juices from the grass, leaving yellow patches. To check for chinch bugs, cut both ends off a coffee can, push it 2 in (5 cm) into the soil at the edge of a yellow spot, and fill with water. Within a few minutes, the chinch bugs will float to the surface.
CONTROL Reduce the thatch on your lawn, use endophyte-enhanced grass cultivars, spot treat with insecticidal soap or pyrethrin.

Sod webworm A small, spotted green caterpillar that munches at night on grass roots, crowns, and leaves, leaving irregular brown patches in its wake. The adult moths fly about lawns with a signature jerky motion. They lay their eggs in the grass in early spring.
CONTROL In most cases, a good dose of fertilizer will help the grass outgrow the damage. *Bacillus thuringiensis* (BT) is effective to kill the caterpillars when they are young, or drench the soil with Steinernema, a parasitic nematode. Also choose endophyte-enhanced grass seed.

Armyworm This southern pest chews grass blades down to the crowns, leaving bare spots. They are a particular problem on Bermuda grass when the weather is cool and wet. Prolific breeders, they can produce as many as six generations in one year.
CONTROL Overseed dead patches with endophyte-enhanced seed. Spray young caterpillars with *Bacillus thuringiensis* var. *kurstaki* or parasitic nematodes.

Slugs These slimy-bodied pests are less of a problem on lawns than for large-leaved plants
CONTROL Keep the grass relatively short to prevent them from damaging turf.

COMMON SLUG

5

COMMON LAWN PESTS

Spider mites Tiny, eight-legged creatures, spider mites suck the juices from grass blades, turning them straw-colored. An infestation can kill large areas of your lawn.
CONTROL Since spider mites thrive on poorly fed lawns that are drought-stressed, your best defense is to keep your lawn properly fertilized and well-watered. If they continue to be a problem, spray insecticidal soap.

Billbugs A pest for northern lawns, particularly Kentucky bluegrass, the grub larvae feed on stems, tunneling into the soil when it gets hot and switching their menu to grass roots. Indications of a problem are yellow and brown patches in the grass and hollowed-out blades filled with a sawdust-like material.
CONTROL Cultural controls include keeping the lawn aerated, topdressing with organic matter, watering deeply, and removing thatch. When reseeding, opt for resistant bluegrass cultivars such as 'Park,' 'Arista,' 'Delta,' and

'NuDarf' or choose a seed blend that includes endophyte-enhanced ryegrass and fescue. In a pinch, apply rotenone.

Mole crickets
A serious lawn pest in the south, particularly on bahia grass, these insects earn their name from their shovel-like feet which they use for tunneling under lawns. There they feed on the roots, causing the grass to wilt and brown, creating irregular streaks.
CONTROL Encourage a deep root system on your lawn and keep thatch to a minimum. Research suggests that the parasitic nematode *Steinernema scaperisci* is a potent predator, as are ground beetles.

Moles These are among the most troublesome lawn pests. The amount of damage they do is staggering and they are very difficult to control. They are small mammals with large, spadelike front paws for digging and very dense, velvet-textured black fur. They are perfectly adapted for a life tunneling beneath the ground in search of

the earthworms and insects that form their food. Unfortunately, the debris from their tunneling is pushed out on to the surface of the lawn as large soil hills. The gallery of runs the moles produce may be near enough to the surface to be visible as ridges. The runs may even collapse, exposing open tunnels. Spring and fall are the main periods of mole activity. Other animals causing similar damage include mice, voles, and gophers.
CONTROL Moles feed on grubs in the lawn. If you solve the grub problem, the odds are good that the moles will go elsewhere. Traps and poisons have only limited success. New moles often move in to the territory of any that have been killed, and cause further trouble by altering and extending the existing runs. Various deterrents involving strong-smelling substances or sonic devices are not consistently reliable, although some gardeners find them useful. Dogs and cats may sometimes catch moles as they come near to the surface when making their hills.

5

COMMON LAWN PESTS

Often, the best course of action is to sweep out molehills and repair obvious tunnels by returfing or reseeding, as necessary, but otherwise to leave the mole alone. Once a mole has established its territory and set out a gallery of runs, the tunneling and molehill production will stop. If he is disturbed he is likely to continue tunneling, causing further damage.

Dogs Dogs can sometimes cause damage by digging up the lawn, but the most difficult problem to deal with is that of urination. Females are the culprits; they squat on the lawn to urinate and the scorching effect leaves circles of dead grass.
CONTROL Copiously watering the affected area straight away helps if you happen to catch a dog in the act. Otherwise the only answer is to reseed or returf affected areas (see p. 48). To avoid further problems, train dogs to urinate in an area away from the lawn that has been set aside for the purpose.

Rabbits In country gardens that border fields, wild rabbits can be a major nuisance. The damage they cause to trees, shrubs, and other plants is usually the main problem, but they can also disfigure lawns by burrowing. Rabbits that are kept as pets may also damage your lawn if allowed to roam freely.
CONTROL Repair damage to lawns by reseeding or returfing. Chemical deterrents are available to discourage wild rabbits from entering your garden, although these do not always work. If rabbits are a persistent problem, wire fencing to keep them out may be the only answer. You need to bury this at least 12 in (30 cm) into the soil all around the perimeter of your property, preferably forming a U-shaped loop underground.

Other wild animals Damage by birds and other wild animals is usually caused when they are searching out insect pests that live in the turf; if possible, take measures to control the insect pests (see pp. 92–93). Various chemical deterrents may be used against wild animals – seek advice from your local garden center.

DOMESTIC RABBIT

COMMON LAWN DISEASES

Dollar spot A fungus that attacks grasses used on golf greens as well as underfed lawns stressed by drought and poor drainage. The lawn dies in circular patches about 4–6 in (10–15 cm) in diameter that can spread and merge to form irregular dead areas. Grass blades have light tan bands with reddish brown margins.
CONTROL Aerate lawn, top-dress with sifted compost, and apply a high-nitrogen fertilizer such as seaweed extract. Overseed dead patches with improved, resistant cultivars such as bluegrass 'Adelphi,' perennial ryegrass 'Manhattan III,' and fine fescue 'Reliant.'

Fairy ring Most common in soils high in woody organic material such as dead tree roots or stumps, fairy ring is a group of fungi spawned by natural decay. You will notice circles or semicircles of dark green grass, often with mushrooms sprouting.
CONTROL Keep the lawn properly fertilized and dethatch if the thatch layer grows too thick. Aerate the lawn to improve water penetration. Use a wetting agent when you water the infected area to help the water soak in deeply.

Fusarium blight A problem for Kentucky bluegrass in the hot days of late summer and early fall. Indicated by 2–6 in (5–15 cm) disks of wilted turf that turn reddish brown.
CONTROL Water-stressed lawns that have been overfed in midsummer are particularly prone. Water deeply, using a wetting agent if necessary, and raise the mowing height. Do not fertilize in summer. Rake out diseased areas and replant with resistant bluegrass cultivars such as 'Adelphi,' 'Columbia,' 'Enmundi,' 'Parade,' 'Sydsport,' and 'Vantage.'

Fusarium patch (pink snow mold) Light tan or rusty brown circular patches gradually grow as big as 2 ft (60 cm) in diameter. The disease blossoms during cool, moist, cloudy weather, usually between fall and spring.
CONTROL Boost cool-season grass vitality with a slow-release nitrogen feeding in fall. Rake away leaves and other debris that may collect on lawn during winter. Also rake to remove damaged grass.

Red thread Most likely to occur in spring and fall when the temperatures are between 60°F (16°C) and 75°F (24°C), this disease is common in the Pacific Northwest and Atlantic Northeast where foggy, moist air is a climatic feature. Red or pink threadlike strands of fungi grow from the grass blade until the infected area eventually turns tan-colored. It targets slow-growing, nitrogen-deficient lawns, especially fine fescues and some perennial ryegrasses.
CONTROL Acid infertile soil encourages the disease. Apply organic fertilizer and top-dress the lawn to the improve the soil. Add ground limestone to raise the pH to between 6 and 7.

Rust As the name suggests, rust is a fungus with spores that coat the grass blades making them a rusty orange color.

5

COMMON LAWN DISEASES

Conditions that favor the fungus are compacted soil, low fertility, shade, and dry, hot weather. In other words, it attacks a stressed lawn.

CONTROL Choose rust-resistant grass cultivars, aerate soil, trim or thin tree branches to increase light levels, give the lawn a high nitrogen boost such as liquid seaweed, mow regularly and collect the clippings, and water in the morning so the grass will dry quickly.

Typhula blight (gray snow mold)
Most common when an early, wet snow falls on unfrozen ground, Typhula blight also tends to develop where snow has been piled in high drifts. Symptoms include matted patches of turf covered with gray, moldy mycelium and rust-colored fungal bodies attached to the infected grass blades and crowns.

CONTROL Do not fertilize too late during the fall otherwise the new growth will not harden off before cold weather. Avoid piling snow high on the lawn and walking on snow-covered grass. Rake the lawn in early spring to help it dry out.

SOLUTIONS FOR PROBLEM PATCHES

POSSIBLE CAUSE	PREVENTION
Worm casts or molehills flattened over grass	Sweep out or remove before mowing.
Scalping	Adjust mower blades to correct height; level high spots in lawn.
Excess wear	Redirect traffic; find alternative surface (e.g. matting under play equipment, hard path etc).
Death of large or spreading weeds after herbicide treatment	Prevention not possible, but resow with grass before new weeds colonize.

5

TURF GRASS
REINFORCEMENT

SOLUTIONS FOR PROBLEM PATCHES

POSSIBLE CAUSE	PREVENTION
Disease	Identify and treat appropriately (see pp. 95–97).
Dog urine	Restrict dog's access to lawn. Water affected areas copiously as soon as possible.
Walking on lawn recently treated with lawn sand	Keep off the lawn until rain has fallen or watering has taken place (within two days of application).
Walking on frosted grass	Keep off the lawn in frosty weather.
Over-application of weed killer/fertilizer	Check application rates; check that equipment is correctly adjusted; avoid overlapping treated strips; take care at ends of rows when turning.
Drought	Water grass thoroughly before it shows signs of stress.
Oil or fuel spills from machinery	Do not refuel, oil, or make adjustments to mowers and other machinery on the lawn. Move them to a hard surface.

GAS MOWER

5

MOWING PROBLEMS

Some lawn problems are caused by incorrect mowing techniques and defective lawn mowers. Have your lawn mower serviced annually and look after it properly (see p. 59) to maintain optimal performance. Mowing mistakes are not difficult to identify if you know what to look for, and most are easy to put right by modifying your technique.

RIBBING

The problem of ribbing is sometimes caused by reel mowers. It is identified by the ragged, torn tips of grass blades that appear at right angles to the direction of cut. One cause is using a lawn mower that has too few blades to the cylinder. The more blades a reel mower has, the finer the cut: this is because the rapidly revolving blades "nibble" the grass in small, sharp bites. For lawn mowers with relatively few blades, each blade takes a proportionately larger bite of grass, with the result that some of the grass is torn rather than cut cleanly. The length of cut also varies.

Ribbing may also be caused by a damaged, blunt, or misaligned blade, by allowing the grass to grow too long, or mowing when the grass is too wet. Check the blades on your lawn mower regularly, and repair or replace any blunt or damaged ones. Increase the frequency of mowing (to two or three times a week in summer, as necessary), first allowing any dew or rain to evaporate. Small amounts of moisture may be removed with a besom.

WASHBOARDING

If turf is routinely mowed in the same direction, a washboarding effect of wavelike ridges sometimes develops on the lawn surface, at right angles to the direction of cut. This problem usually is caused by powered lawn mowers. It is an easy habit to fall into, since it somehow seems more logical to have stripes running up and down the lawn rather than across it. To avoid washboarding, and to improve the lawn's general appearance, remember to alternate the direction each time you cut, mowing at right angles to the previous direction of cut.

GRAIN

This problem is caused by repeatedly mowing in the same direction. The term "grain" describes grass stems and leaves that grow horizontally rather than vertically, forming an obvious pattern with all the shoots pointing in the same direction. Grain

Warning

Take care when using rotary mowers, since they may fling objects such as stones, or other heavy objects left lying on the surface of the lawn, over considerable distances. Stones and other debris may be propelled at great force by the action of the mower blades, causing serious injury to bystanders, and possibly damaging nearby property. Always walk across the lawn before mowing, removing any debris before you begin. It is also wise to moderate the speed of the mower and ignore all distractions, so that you may concentrate on the job in hand.

may be prevented by alternating the direction of cut, and raking the grass before mowing so that the shoots stand up to meet the mower blades.

SCALPING

If the mower blades are set too low, you will remove all the green portion of the grass, leaving only the lower brown stems or even bare earth. This is known as scalping. It may also occur on high spots on uneven lawns. Scalping is prevented by leveling any high spots (see p. 51) and adjusting the mower blades throughout the season to give the correct height of cut (see p. 61).

TURNING DAMAGE

Be careful when turning the lawn mower at the end of each mowing strip, particularly if you use a heavy powered mower. A tight, spinning turn may leave characteristic "arcs" on the turf where the grass has been bruised. Try to make a slower loop when turning with your mower to prevent causing unsightly and possibly harmful damage around the edges of the lawn.

MOWING STRIPES
By mowing with a rear roller attachment on your lawn mower you can achieve satisfying stripes in a regular pattern across the lawn.

5

WEATHER DAMAGE

Turf is surprisingly resilient and will usually survive short periods of drought or heavy rainfall. Extreme weather conditions such as heavy snowfall and strong winds may present more of a problem, although all but the severest weather damage is easily remedied.

EXCESSIVE RAIN

Prolonged periods of heavy rain have a number of detrimental effects on grass. Persistent rain usually goes hand in hand with lack of sunshine, resulting in temperature and light quality being reduced to below ideal levels for good growth. If the grass roots are waterlogged for extended periods, the grass will die. A moist atmosphere also encourages the development of fungal diseases (see pp. 95–96). Wet soil is easily compacted by foot traffic, and the grass itself is more easily damaged when it is wet. Ensure drainage is adequate, aerating the grass if necessary (pp. 74–75), and keep off the lawn during wet weather.

DROUGHT

After a period without water, grass will wilt and eventually turn brown and become dormant. Thorough watering before the grass starts to show signs of stress will help to keep the lawn looking green and attractive (see pp. 66–69). The high temperatures and intense sun often associated with drought, may also damage the grass, newly sown lawns, or recently laid sod. Regular watering helps to regulate the temperature of both turf and soil.

DROUGHT DAMAGE
New-laid sod is especially prone to drying out during hot summers. Without regular watering, the grass starts to wilt and then turns brown.

5

FROST

In itself, frost does not usually damage cool-season grasses (apart from newly germinated seedlings). If frosted grass is crushed by walking across it, for example, it will die. Always keep traffic off the lawn during frosty conditions.

SNOW

A covering of snow actually insulates the turf against extreme cold, but the moist, cool microclimate it provides tends to encourage the spread of certain diseases, such as fusarium patch, or snow mold (see p. 95). As the snow begins to melt it may also cause waterlogging unless the underlying drainage is good.

WIND

Grass tips may be scorched in hot, windy conditions, especially on exposed sites. Newly sown lawns also may be badly affected as the wind can whip away the finely worked soil on the surface and dry out the seeds within minutes. Protect them with a temporary windbreak by erecting a permanent screen in spots that have chronic wind. Winds in coastal areas may carry damaging salt spray. Choose salt-tolerant varieties of grass such as Bermuda grass and St. Augustine.

THE LAWN IN WINTER
A covering of frost on the lawn's surface glistens in the winter sunshine, while topiary hedges and sculptures cast interesting shadows.

5

SHADE

Grass is difficult to establish in the shade of overhanging trees or nearby buildings, since the cool, moist conditions and low light levels provide poor growing conditions. Turf that grows in shade usually lacks vigor, and is less able to shrug off diseases and the effects of adverse weather conditions. It will also have poor wearing qualities. As a result, turf in shaded areas is likely to be thin and patchy, with regular pathways soon becoming bare.

CULTURAL CONTROLS

■ **Mowing and feeding** Mow shaded lawns with the blades set higher than for those in full sun, and keep foot traffic to a bare minimum. Feed the grass regularly to promote strong growth but do not use a high-nitrogen fertilizer too often, since this will encourage the growth of very soft, disease-prone shoots.

■ **Dealing with moss** Moss is much better suited to shady conditions than grass, and moss proliferation can become a serious nuisance on shaded lawns. In areas of extreme shade, however, a covering of moss may be beneficial, since it will at least maintain a form of green carpet, a point to bear in mind before trying to eradicate it (see p.73).

■ **Reducing shade** Where possible, reduce shade by removing the lower branches of trees and thinning the crowns to allow more light to penetrate to the lawn below. Bear in mind that if you decide to cut down a tree in your garden, you might need to get permission, since a local regulation could exist to protect certain trees in your area. If it is not possible to remove or reduce the shade cast by trees, or if the shade is caused by some other immovable obstruction, such as a building, select a shade-tolerant seed mixture (or seeded turf) for the lawn.

SHADE-TOLERANT SEED MIX

5

GRASSES FOR SHADE

COOL-SEASON
Fine fescue: 'Aurora,' 'Jamestown II,' 'Reliant,' 'Scaldis,' 'SR3100,' 'SR5000'
Kentucky bluegrass: 'Georgetown'
Perennial ryegrass: 'Advent,' 'APM,' 'Express,' Fiesta II,' 'Manhattan II'
Tall fescue: 'Apache,' 'Arid,' 'Bonanza II,' 'Duster,' 'Mustang,' 'Pixie,' 'Rebel Jr.'

WARM-SEASON
Bahia grass: 'Argentine,' 'Pensacola'
Centipede grass common: 'Oaklawn,' 'Tennessee Hardy,' 'Centennial'
St. Augustine grass: common, 'Raleigh'
Zoysia: 'Belair'

Alternatives to a grass lawn

Dispensing with grass 104
Looks at the alternatives to grass for play areas, and how ground-cover plants, paved areas, and gravel can all be used to good effect

Non-grass lawns 106
Explains how mat-forming plants can be used to simulate grass, and discusses the merits of thyme and chamomile for lawns

Wild flower meadows 110
Suggests ways to create and maintain a wild flower meadow in place of a grass lawn

ALTERNATIVES TO A GRASS LAWN

A lawn is the most labor-intensive ground cover available to gardeners. In contrast, most other ground covers need little or no maintenance once they are established. Some, such as crown vetch, honeysuckle, and germander, should be mowed or pruned once or twice a year for the best appearance, but that care is minimal compared with a lawn's requirements. As for weeding, a densely growing ground cover should choke out all but the most persistent of troublesome weeds.

Paved surfaces are another option instead of grass. In mild climates, a paved patio or terrace furnished with tables and chairs becomes an extension of the house, and even in regions with harsh winters, patios are viable as "outdoor rooms" for several months during the summer. Although the initial outlay for a paved patio is high, once it is installed, the area becomes virtually cost-free, needing no maintenance other than the occasional sweeping or hosing off.

DISPENSING WITH GRASS

Grass is by far the most commonly used plant for lawns, and with good reason. It is easy to grow, surprisingly resilient, and relatively straightforward to maintain. However, there are occasions when grass may not be the first choice as a method of covering the ground. You may not want to spend your leisure time on lawn maintenance, or perhaps you find grass dull and want something with more year-round interest.

CONSIDERING ALTERNATIVES

Many busy homeowners want an attractive garden, but one that takes a minimum of weekly maintenance so they can spend their spare time on other activities. The regular and somewhat tedious care that a lawn requires is more than they want to commit to. In addition, some garden situations are simply not suitable for lawn cultivation. Deep shade or inaccessible spots in the garden where you cannot get the mower are two examples. If you have many changes in level in your garden that are connected by steps, the task of getting the lawn mower up and down also is a deterrent.

Fortunately, there are many alternatives to the traditional lawn that are attractive substitutes. In fact

CHESHIRE PINK GRAVEL

planting a small lawn as a special garden feature in conjunction with paved spaces, other ground covers, and beds and borders adds to the overall interest of the garden.

■ **Paved surfaces** A well-planned hardscape extends the living space of your home. Choice of materials for paving has grown enormously in the past few years, and today there are paving materials available that will fit almost any budget. On the high end is traditional brick as well as stone products imported from around the world. Companies have introduced interlocking pavers that are easy to lay as a do-it-yourself

COLORFUL ALTERNATIVES
Artificial grass (top), made from hard-wearing plastic or nylon, or decorative mulches, such as cocoa hulls (bottom), suit children's play areas.

project, and the basic, inexpensive concrete slab can be tinted for added interest or molded to look like bricks or stones.

■ **Loose materials** In areas of deep shade or where nothing will grow because of a shallow-rooted tree or extremely poor soil, mulch is ideal. It covers the ground, giving a tidy, groomed look to the space. Gravel or cobblestones are very attractive, especially if you are creating a "dry riverbed." You might combine stones of different colors and textures to make an abstract design in a dry garden. Among the many organic possibilities are shredded or chipped bark, cocoa hulls, and pine needles.

■ **Ground cover plants** In addition to the traditional, spreading plants that hug the ground such as ivies,

ice plants, and periwinkles, ground covers can include any low-growing plant that can be effectively massed to cover the ground. Consider mass planting medium-sized hostas, daylilies, ferns, or small shrubs such as deutzia or rockspray cotoneaster *(Cotoneaster horizontalis)*.

Ground covers are a great option in heavily shaded areas. Try growing bergenia, green and gold *(Chrysogonum virginianum)*, sweet woodruff, European wild ginger *(Asarum europaeum)*, or yellow archangel *(Lamiastrum galeobdolon)*. These plants are valued for their ability to spread aggressively in all but the most inhospitable soil. Some ground covers tolerate light foot traffic. Choose scented plants, such as thymes, which will release their fragrance when they are crushed underfoot.

CHILDREN'S PLAY AREA
Wood chips are a good choice below a children's swing set, where grass would soon become worn. This kind of surface will also cushion the inevitable falls.

DECKING

The natural texture and appearance of timber decking make it very appealing. Use timber that has been pressure treated with preservative. Site a wooden patio or verandah in a sunny spot so that it dries quickly after rain and does not get slippery.

6

NON-GRASS LAWNS

Certain ground-cover plants may be used to form a dense, low-growing, ground-hugging mat that bears a close resemblance to a grass lawn. The two best known plants in this category are sweet-smelling chamomile, which is long established as a lawn plant, and thyme, also with aromatic leaves, but there are other possibilities, too. Chamomile and thyme are discussed in detail on pages 108–109.

MAT-FORMING PLANTS

If the definition of a lawn is a low-growing carpet that is evergreen, covers the ground densely, and will take at least light foot traffic, there are several plants to fit the bill. *Leptinella* (previously known as *Cotula*) forms a tight, dense mat of deep green, ferny leaves that have good wearing qualities.

Particular species of some plants have been specially selected for growing as turf plants. *Dichondra micrantha* is a creeping perennial

CHECKERBOARD EFFECT
To create this effect, use two or three different species or varieties of ground cover plants to create a non-grass lawn as a "living patchwork."

6

with bright green, round or kidney-shaped leaves. Although *Dichondra* will withstand frost, it grows best in warm climates. It prefers well drained but moisture-retentive soils (watering is necessary in dry spells) and will tolerate some shade. Like *Leptinella*, it will withstand moderate foot traffic. Both *Leptinella* and *Dichondra* may be mown to produce a close, dense sward.

Other ground-cover plants that tolerate light foot traffic include *Potentilla neumanniana* 'Nana' (*P. verna* 'Nana'), *Sagina subulata*, *Ajuga reptans*, *Armeria maritima*, and *Lysimachia nummularia*.

> **TIP**
>
> Some gardeners dislike the large block of solid color created by single-species lawns. If you want to make an eye-catching tapestry of ground cover plants, choose varieties and species with similar growth rates – otherwise one species will quickly dominate and crowd out all the others. Good possibilities include creeping thyme plants such as mother-of-thyme (*Thymus serpyllum*), both pink- and white-flowering varieties, and woolly thyme (*T. pseudolanuginosus*).

ERADICATING WEEDS

One of the drawbacks of using any non-grass plants to form a "lawn" is that you cannot use selective weed killers to control weeds, since the lawn would also suffer the effects of any treatment. The only option is to hand weed or use herbicides to give spot treatments. Competition from weeds can therefore be a major problem, especially when you are trying to establish the lawn.

It is essential to prepare the site thoroughly before you create the lawn. Take extra care to remove all traces of perennial weeds. Once the soil has been prepared, leave it fallow for two to three weeks to allow the weed seeds that have been brought to the surface to germinate. The resulting flush of weeds can then be hoed off or treated with a suitable weed killer, such as glyphosate, before planting. When planting, disturb the soil as little as possible to avoid bringing other weed seeds up to the surface of the lawn.

SCENTED THYME
The evergreen leaves of mat-forming *Thymus* give off a powerful scent; they are traditionally used in herbal medicine and also for cooking.

CORSICAN MINT
Low-growing *Mentha requienii* spreads widely but needs shade and moist soil. When crushed, the leaves have a strong peppermint fragrance.

6

CHAMOMILE

Chamomile has a long history and was particularly popular in England during Elizabethan times. The species that is used for lawns is *Chamaemelum nobile* (formerly *Anthemis nobilis*), zones 6–9. A hardy perennial with bright green, deeply cut, ferny leaves, it grows to a height of around 4 in (10 cm). When bruised, the leaves have a strong, sweet smell that is reminiscent of ripe apples. The plants are spreading and invasive. *C. nobile* bears small, white, daisy flowers, with white petals and yellow centers, in late spring and early summer. The best chamomile to use for lawns is the cultivar *C.* 'Treneague,' which does not flower and is less invasive than the species.

■ **Cultivation** Chamomile likes a free-draining but moisture-retentive soil and an open, sunny position. It can be grown from seed broadcast in mid-spring but this method makes weed control very difficult. It is better to sow seed in containers, then transplant the seedlings to the lawn. *C.* 'Treneague' is more expensive than *C. nobile* but is much more reliable as a lawn plant. Since *C.* 'Treneague' does not produce flowers, it cannot be grown from seed and must be propagated from cuttings. In spring, prepare the site thoroughly to eradicate weeds, setting out the young plants 4–6 in (10–15 cm) apart each way.

Water the new plants as necessary in dry spells, and hand-pull any weeds. As the plants establish, mow (on a high setting) or clip the plants to keep them neat and dense and to prevent *C. nobile* flowering. Damp, cool weather often harms chamomile, so you may need to replace some plants each year to fill gaps.

THYME

Like chamomile, thyme has aromatic leaves that give off a pleasantly fresh fragrance when trodden on. The plants produce a rolling, undulating sward and carry attractive flowers in summer. The creeping, mat-forming thymes are the ones to use for lawns; among these are *Thymus serpyllum*, *T. caespititius*, *T. pseudolanuginosus*, *T. praecox*, and *T. doerfleri*, zones 5–10. They are spreading plants with wiry stems and small, oval leaves that are sometimes variegated cream or gold. Small clusters of lipped white, purple or pink flowers are carried on short stems in summer. The flowers are particularly popular with bees. Lots of different cultivars are available, with a variety of fragrance, habit, and foliage and flower color. *T.* 'Elfin,' *T.* 'Pink Chintz,' *T.* 'Annie Hall,' *T.* 'Bressingham,' and *T.* 'Minus' are all good choices for lawns.

■ **Cultivation** Free-draining soil and a sunny position suit thyme well. Once established, it adapts well to dry conditions. Raise young plants or buy them in spring, setting them out about 6 in (15 cm) apart: the exact spacing depends on the cultivar. Keep the plants moist while they establish, and hand weed regularly.

The flowers produced during the summer usually attract large numbers of bees, making it unwise to walk on the thyme at flowering time. Mow over or clip back the plants when they have finished flowering. This shearing gets rid of the unattractive dead flower heads and promotes new leafy growth.

CHAMOMILE LAWN
A gently undulating sward of bright green chamomile sets off the foliage colors of the ornamental shrubs growing at its edge.

6

6

WILD FLOWER MEADOWS

A meadow is any kind of grassland. It can be wet, dry, or very dry (in which case it would be classified as a prairie). A meadow is a dynamic planting situation that supports a wide variety of vegetation and animal life. Once established, meadows require a minimum of maintenance. If you opt for native plants, or plants that are well adapted to your climate and soil, little or no extra watering is needed.

CREATING A WILD FLOWER MEADOW

Comprised of sun-loving plants, a meadow needs a minimum of six hours of direct sun daily. With that in mind, choose a sunny location, perhaps an outer edge of your garden, a transition space between two areas, or even an island bed in the middle of a lawn in lieu of the more standard herbaceous display.

Remember that many communities have decades-old "weed" laws banning grass that is taller than a prescribed height. These laws were enacted long before the recent resurgence in interest in natural gardening. If a weed law exists in your community, you may need to get permission from the city before you embark on a creating a meadow.

■ **Preparing the site** Begin by eliminating existing vegetation and then test the soil to determine if it

ACCESS THROUGH A MEADOW
A mown grass path around a meadow improves access, inviting you in and bringing the wild flowers and grasses within reach.

needs any amendments. Generally an application of lime and fertilizer is helpful. Although meadow plants enjoy a starvation diet, most need soil that is not too heavy so it drains well and is aerated. Early in spring, as soon as the ground is workable, turn the soil to a depth of 4 in (10 cm), water, and wait two or three weeks for weeds to sprout. Then pull, hoe, or rototill the weed seedlings.

■ **Sowing seed** Once the ground is prepared, sow your seeds. If you are buying your seeds by weight, expect to need 5–20 lb per acre (2–9 kg per 0.4 ha), depending on the species. Certain seed types weigh much less than others. Rake the area lightly to give the seeds good contact with the soil, water, and then apply an organic mulch, such as a 1–2-in (2.5–5-cm)

layer of straw. If the ground slopes, stop erosion and seed drift by laying down a netting made of a biodegradable material such as cotton string.

Water daily (unless it rains) for the first three weeks, then twice a week for the next month. Once established, your meadow should need no extra water.

■ **Maintaining your meadow** An established meadow should be fairly self-sustaining. Mow once a year, either in late summer after the seeds have dropped or, if you want to enjoy the dried grasses through the winter, in early spring. If you mow in the fall, leave the clippings to encourage species to reseed and to serve as a mulch through winter. If you mow in early spring, rake away most of the clippings.

CHOOSING WILD FLOWER MIXTURES

A meadow is comprised of two plant categories: grasses and forbs (which are nongrass herbaceous plants). Generally a balanced meadow with multiseason interest includes:

• Base grass or nurse crop of nonaggressive grasses such as chewings fescue, sheep fescue, or buffalograss for soil stabilization.

• Bulbs such as naturalized narcissi, irises, camassia, and allium.

• Biennials such as Queen Anne's lace and verbascum.

• Annuals such as poppies, chicory, California poppies, and cornflower.

• Perennials such as daylilies, golden rod, and butterfly weed.

WILD POPPIES

6

INDEX

ACKNOWLEDGMENTS

Photography: Steven Wooster p. 8, p. 9, p. 12, p. 13, p. 40, p. 57, p. 67, p. 74, p. 91; Hayter Ltd p. 97; David Askam, Garden Picture Library p. 100; Steven Wooster p.101, p. 106, p. 109, 9p.110, p.111
Equipment: Porta-kneel supplied by NBS Sports and Leisure p. 28; lawnmowers supplied by Atco-Qualcast Ltd, Suffolk p. 37, p. 55, p.59; Tuff Turf supplied by Supreme Concrete Ltd p. 96; and NeverBend range of garden tools supplied by Spear and Jackson.
Thanks to Country Gardens, Tring, Herts; Oliver Blacklock; Leslie Smith; Michael Spilling; Tim Stansfield; and Sally Wilton